The
Lord's Prayer
for today

Derek Prime

DayOnepublications

All scripture quotations are from The New International Version © 1973, 1978, 1984,
International Bible Society. Published by Hodder and Stoughton.

ISBN 0 902548 68 9

Published by Day One Publications
6 Sherman Road, Bromley, Kent BR1 3JH

Designed by Steve Devane and printed by Clifford Frost Ltd, Wimbledon SW19 2SE

The Lord's Prayer

Our Father in heaven,

hallowed be your name,

your kingdom come,

your will be done on earth as it is in heaven.

Give us today our daily bread.

Forgive us our debts, as we also have
forgiven our debtors.

And lead us not into temptation,

but deliver us from the evil one,

for yours is the kingdom and the power and
the glory forever.

Amen.

The
Lord's Prayer
for today

By way of explanation

Every book begins with a seed thought. Soon after the invitation came to give Bible ministry at the 1993 Caister meetings of the Fellowship of Independent Evangelical Churches, the Lord's Prayer came clearly into focus as an appropriate subject. Some thirty-six years before, I was called to the pastorate of Lansdowne Evangelical Free Church in south London. The first series of sermons I prepared for the ministry there were on the Lord's Prayer. I can remember working at them during the summer holiday preceding my ordination in October 1957. Strangely perhaps I never preached another series on the Lord's Prayer in subsequent years. As I studied the prayer afresh for Caister 1993 I wished that I had!

Both Brian Edwards and John Blanchard shared in Caister that year, and John Roberts represented Day One Publications. As the four of us chatted together, Brian mentioned that he wanted to write something on the Ten Commandments, and John that he had had in view for some time writing on either the Beatitudes or the Lord's Prayer. John Roberts suggested that we might join together and produce a trilogy on these three important parts of the Bible. Hence an early morning breakfast together in 1994 and some months later the manuscripts were in production. It is good to write in fellowship with others and I am grateful to the Lord for the privilege, for 'From him and through him and to him are all things. To him be the glory for ever!' (Romans 11:36).

Introduction

Why the emphasis in our title upon **The Lord's Prayer for today**? The grounds for the stress upon **today** are twofold: neglect and relevance. First, the Lord's Prayer is in danger of being neglected. It would not appear to be used much by Christians in private prayer, and it does not find widespread use in corporate worship as once it did.

In some parts of the Church there has been a turning away from much that is traditional in corporate worship: much of what was customary or conventional is regarded as synonymous with what is out of date and irrelevant. The announcement in public worship 'Let us pray together the prayer our Lord Jesus taught his disciples' would sound to some to belong to a former era. Because the prayer has not been regularly used, not everyone may even know the words. The problem may be increased by the language in which the prayer is usually couched, so that when prayed in public, its language contrasts with that which has become usual in prayer, where 'thou', 'thee' and 'thine' have been replaced by 'you', 'your' and 'yours'.

Another factor is the contemporary pattern of a number of people sharing in the leadership of public worship. Seldom may a person take the same part two weeks running, and so the inclusion of the Lord's Prayer may simply be overlooked for a few Sundays and in no time it becomes the habit not to include it.

Observations on a subject like this are necessarily subjective, and inevitably influenced by personal experience, but it does seem that even prayer itself in gatherings of Christians is in danger of neglect. Often the prayer that is offered early in a service is a prayer of 'worship' - perhaps at the beginning or during the first part of a service - and from then on there may be no expression of repentance and confession of sin, and little or no intercession for the Church and the world at large.

To reinstate the Lord's Prayer can only be beneficial. It reminds us at its very beginning that true worship of God arises from a living relationship with him as our Father through our Lord Jesus, and a preoccupation with his Name (his revealed character), his kingdom and his will. We need these emphases **today**, as much as the Church has ever done.

Second, we emphasise **The Lord's Prayer for today** because of its relevance. As the only pattern prayer the Lord Jesus provided, it is timeless in purpose and function. It indicates how we are to pray throughout our life in this present world. Enduring in its principles, it needs to be interpreted afresh for every generation. Its truths do not change, but their application may.

For example, the truth of God's Fatherhood of his spiritual children is glorious, but the present down-grading of human fatherhood, and the sad experiences so many have of it, demand careful explanation of God's unique and perfect Fatherhood. Tragically, some have no happy experience of human fatherhood and we need to be aware of that when we explain God's Fatherhood, and to handle the matter sensitively.

The concept of God's Name and its importance are foreign to contemporary ways of thinking. We use names casually, whereas the Bible never does. That also needs to be explained.

Political and social movements have employed the concept of God's kingdom in ways different from our Lord Jesus, and we need to recapture its proper use.

God's will is sometimes spoken of as if it were arbitrary and capricious; or it is, on the other hand, identified with material prosperity and personal affluence. We need to rescue it from such errors and to discover the joy of living both for God's will and under it.

Whilst most of us who read this book live without hunger, a large proportion of the world's population does not. The petition 'Give us today our daily bread' can be prayed with integrity only as we relate ourselves seriously to others' need of bread as well as our own.

Sin and temptation are words which are absent from popular vocabulary; they are distinctly unfashionable. The stock in trade of contemporary entertainment is the enjoyment of unrestrained human desires. Holiness - still God's priority for his children - cannot be pursued unless sin is seen to be sin, and temptation is seen as something we are to flee from or resolutely resist. As we proceed, I hope we shall increasingly appreciate the treasure of instruction and guidance the Lord Jesus gives for **today** in his gift of **The Lord's Prayer.**

A TREASURE TO GIVE NEW CHRISTIANS

The instruction of new Christians provides a further powerful reason for focusing upon the Lord's Prayer. What should we teach new Christians? What do they need to know in order to live the Christian life? I would suggest three priority areas of instruction.

First, a Creed is essential - that is to say, a statement of Christian belief in which we identify and affirm the truth about the one true God in whom we trust and the gospel of his Son, Jesus Christ. The New Testament contains several credal statements (e.g. 1 Corinthians 15:3-5; Philippians 2:5-11; 1 Timothy 3:16), and as challenges to God's revealed truth have arisen the Church has provided further declarations of faith. Instructed in God's truth, we know **what** we believe, and **in whom** we believe (2 Timothy 1:12).

Secondly, an understanding of the Ten Commandments and their practical relevance to daily life is vital, especially in a society where people have so lost their way that they think that it is up to individuals to define their own rules. The Ten Commandments perfectly reflect our Maker's character and indicate the moral direction in which he wants our lives to go. They are as necessary for life as bones for the body or rails for a train. Although given under the Old Testament, they remain a permanent guide to our Creator's will. The Lord Jesus did not put aside these instructions, but rather he fulfilled them, and he provides the spiritual resources to obey them.

Thirdly - and here we come to the importance of our present subject - an appreciation of the Lord's Prayer gives unique insight into our new relationship with God through his Son, Jesus Christ. The gospel we believe - defined in the Creed - and the life-style we now want to follow in obedience to his commandments has in view a life of fellowship with God, and that finds its principal expression in prayer.

Our contemporary world is preoccupied with fast and effective communication. I can lift the telephone, dial direct to the other side of the world, and be in touch in seconds. Even as I write and you now read satellites circle the earth, business people speak to one another on mobile phones, computers transmit data to each other, and fax-machines produce almost instant written communication. But no communication is more wonderful - or instant - than prayer. In fact, God anticipates our prayer. He declares of his people's prayers, 'Before they call I will answer; while they are still speaking I will hear' (Isaiah 65:24). His answer is on its way before we call. Nevertheless he requires us to call! The lines of communication between God and ourselves, once established through the gift of salvation in the Lord Jesus, need never break down.

We fail new Christians if we do not teach them how to pray. A major purpose of our Lord Jesus' life and death was that we might be brought to God and thus have this access to God. Prayer is our breath, our spiritual life-line. It is the highest exercise of our souls, an expression of our living relationship with God. For Christians to pray is as natural as breathing. One of the first things the Lord told Ananias about the newly converted Saul, whom he was to welcome into God's family, was, 'He is praying' (Acts 9:11). That was significant: members of God's family do pray.

But that is not to say that prayer is easy. Nothing is more important, and yet nothing is more difficult to maintain. Many battles in our Christian life revolve around giving prayer its rightful place, and knowing how best to use our privilege. Satan tries to keep us from prayer, for he knows that time spent in close prayer fellowship with God on just one day can frustrate the evil plans he has been working at for a long time. He is skilful and well-practised in bringing to mind duties which demand our immediate attention so as to turn us away from prayer. Or if we do pray, he endeavours to make us pray without purpose, or in a mechanical and careless manner. He encourages us to pray to God without first listening to God.

Prayer is an area in which we always have much to learn. In particular, we need to know how to approach God with acceptance. We require directions, rules and helps in prayer because 'we do not know what we ought to pray for' (Romans 8:26). There is a danger that we may ask in the wrong way or for inappropriate things (James 4:3).

If we were invited to Buckingham Palace to be presented to the Queen, or to the White House to meet the President of the United States of America, there would be immediate questions in our minds - matters of etiquette and protocol. When, for example, someone in Britain is admitted to the Privy Council - the Sovereign's closest group of advisers - the ceremony of admission involves kneeling on a red stool, swearing the oath of loyalty to the Crown and kissing the sovereign's hand - and in that required order. Invited to meet the Queen or the President we would be asking, 'How should we enter their presence? What should we say? Are there particular subjects we should speak about? Or, on the other hand, are there topics to avoid?' How much more should we be concerned to know how to approach God! Here the Lord's Prayer comes into its own. The whole of the Bible helps direct our prayers, but this prayer provides the 'how' of prayer - and uniquely so. 'This is how you should pray,' our Saviour said (Matthew 6:9).

Our purpose is to study the Lord's Prayer to ensure that we use it well, and apply the principles it teaches. Although most Christians give lip service to its importance, it is probably one of the least considered parts of the Bible. Martin Luther described the Lord's Prayer as the greatest martyr on earth, because it was used so frequently without thought and feeling, without reverence and faith.

THE DISCIPLES' PRAYER

What we call 'the Lord's Prayer' is the prayer our Lord Jesus Christ taught his disciples. It might be better named, therefore, 'the Disciples' Prayer'. But its familiar name is best kept since it underlines its importance, especially as it is the only prayer the gospels record our Saviour teaching his disciples, and its occurrence in two different contexts in the gospels implies he gave it to them more than once. That there are two different versions indicates we are not to be tied to the actual words, but to the priorities they express. Matthew records it as part of the Sermon on the Mount (Matthew 6:9-13), whereas Luke gives it as Jesus' response to his disciples' request that he should teach them to pray (Luke 11:2-4).

HELPFUL CONTEXTS

Prayer was our Lord's habit and custom - the secret source of his strength (Luke 22:39,43). Luke's context of the giving of the Lord's Prayer points to our Lord's own priority practice of prayer. When the disciples awoke of a morning they invariably found he was already up, seeking his Father's face (Mark 1:35).

He received his Father's guidance as he prayed. After prayer, he decided to move on to other places (Mark 1:38-39). Before choosing and calling the apostles, he spent a night in prayer (Luke 6:12,13). His decision to question the disciples about their understanding of his Messiahship and Divine Sonship was preceded by prayer (Luke 9:18; cf. Matthew 16:13). They could not fail to notice that prayer surrounded the most important events in his ministry. Observing him pray like this prompted their request, 'Lord, teach us to pray, just as John taught his disciples' (Luke 11:1). 'How do you begin?' 'For what do you ask?' These were questions in their minds.

The context of the Lord's Prayer in Matthew's gospel is Jesus' instruction on three subjects: giving to the needy (6:1-4); prayer (6:5-15); and fasting (6:16-18). The emphasis with regard to each is upon sincerity and hiddenness, underlining that godliness is essentially what we are in secret before God, for the chapter begins: 'Be careful not to do your "acts of righteousness" before men, to be seen by them. If you do, you will have no reward from your Father in heaven' (6:1).

True prayer - like genuine giving and fasting - is 'an act of right-eousness' in that it first pleases God and that it has others' good in view as well as our own. We are not to pray only for ourselves; part of prayer's essence is the expression of concern before God for other people.

Private prayer is at its best when done in secret. We are to go into our room, close the door and pray to our unseen Father. Then our Father, who sees what is done in secret, will reward us (Matthew 6:6). Prayer is a God-ward act: it is not to be paraded or put on display, for then human pride easily enters in. Prayer offered with God's pleasure alone in view is always rewarded.

Prayer is not just uttering words to God. The worth of our prayers is not to be judged by their length or eloquence. Their value to God is in their sincerity and harmony with his revealed will. 'Babbling like pagans' (Matthew 6:7) is totally inappropriate. The Lord's Prayer shows what it is to pray according to God's will.

THE DIFFERENCE BETWEEN PRAYERS AND SUPPLICATIONS

The Lord's Prayer illustrates what is meant by 'prayers' in contrast to 'requests' or 'supplications'. The Bible encourages us to 'pray in the Spirit on all occasions with all kinds of prayers and requests' (Ephesians 6:18), indicating a difference between 'prayers' and 'requests'. The distinction is that 'prayers' stand for matters of daily concern, and for which we may often need to pray in a general way because we cannot be dogmatic in our understanding of how God may answer them. The petitions of the Lord's prayer sum up these general issues. 'Requests' or 'supplications', on the other hand, relate to urgent matters that arise. While we may not have to pray daily for an emergency or crisis - which may disappear as quickly as they appear - we do need to pray daily for the subjects upon which the Lord's Prayer focuses.

A PRAYER PATTERN OR TEMPLATE

The Lord's Prayer establishes a foundation upon which to build our requests to God. It is helpful to think of it as a prayer template, or pattern. Joiners make templates to reproduce articles, dressmakers use patterns to make garments of a similar size - and both work with a variety of materials. So the Lord's Prayer provides a variety of prayers and concerns, but always in conformity with the basic pattern our Lord

Jesus provided. It is the only model which our Saviour has given us. We are not bound to its words, but we are tied to its basic content. Our Lord Jesus lays out our legitimate agenda for prayer when we come to our heavenly Father: he tells us what our Father wants us to ask. When we pray this prayer from our hearts we may be sure that we pray according to God's will. As a template it identifies the vital topics and, by the order in which they appear, guides us as to our priorities in prayer. Like a mould it shapes our prayers into an acceptable form.

With the clamouring voices of human need in our ears, we may find ourselves bewildered as to where to begin in our praying: the Lord's Prayer directs us. As we pray these petitions with understanding and in the Spirit, we address the world's deepest distresses and concerns. At the same time they teach us to pray for God's interests - his Name, his kingdom, and his will - before our own personal cares which so easily dominate our thoughts, and, therefore, our prayers.

ITS CORPORATE USE

How should we use this prayer? Should we pray it together? And if so, how frequently? Behind such questions is concern that we should not fall into the danger Jesus warns against of babbling like pagans (Matthew 6:7). The risk of praying the Lord's Prayer without thinking always exists, but that applies to every form of words used in prayer. The Lord's Prayer corrects wordiness and vagueness in prayer.

As well as being a prayer template to guide all our prayers, the prayer itself should be prayed together for that is what Jesus instructed. It certainly became the practice of early Christians, no doubt as a consequence of the apostles' teaching and example. Tertullian (c.160/70-c.215/20) and Cyprian (c.200/10-258), for example, indicate it was the usual prayer of the congregation. No instruction is given about how often we should use it in our worship, and therefore we should not lay down rules. But that it has a place is beyond dispute.

Since it begins 'Our Father', we are encouraged to pray it together as members of his one family. We should use it as often as we can, as long as we enter into it meaningfully. When we feel in danger of merely repeating words, we should put it aside for a while, or better still - as we now try to do - remind ourselves afresh of the truths it teaches. If we avoid using the prayer because of fear of repetitiveness, we rob ourselves of an invaluable gift from God to aid us in our prayers. If, however, we educate ourselves in its significance, we may appreciate it more every time we pray it together.

Chapter 1

Trusting children

'Our Father in heaven'

These are the most meaningful words of the Lord's Prayer. A major benefit of our salvation in Jesus Christ is the privilege of calling God 'Father'. It is amazing that the prayer should begin like this. It might have begun, 'Mighty God', 'Majestic Lord', 'Our Maker', 'Our King', 'Our Protector', 'Our Shepherd' or 'Our Righteous Judge'. To call God 'Father' is a particular benefit of the gospel.

God's Fatherhood is mentioned in the Old Testament. God said to Moses, for example, 'Israel is my firstborn son,' and told him to tell Pharaoh, 'Let my son go, so that he may worship me' (Exodus 4:22,23). The people of Israel are frequently described as God's children - although often rebellious (Deuteronomy 14:1; 32:5; Isaiah 1:4; 30:9; 43:6; 45:11; Jeremiah 31:20; Hosea 2:1; Malachi 2:10). But the joy of the relationship to God as Father bursts forth in its fulness only in the New Testament.

FATHERHOOD OR MOTHERHOOD?

Some rebel against the use of the title 'Father', and go to great lengths to replace it by 'Mother'. In September 1995 the Oxford University Press in America published *The New Testament and Psalms: an Inclusive Version* in which God is omni-sexual, and the Lord's Prayer begins, 'Our Father-Mother in Heaven.' Campaigners for such changes suggest that male-domination of society has influenced the way in which God's character has been understood in the past. While sometimes that may have been the case, the Bible is absolutely clear in its declaration of God's Fatherhood.

Three responses must be made to this desire to change the way in which we speak to God, and think of him. First, we dare not tamper with God's self-revelation in order to please contemporary society's demands which do not accept the Bible's authority and inspiration. The Bible consistently uses the title 'Father' as the distinguishing name of the First Person of the Trinity. Secondly, God does sometime choose to use the picture of motherhood to describe his relationship to his people (Isaiah 49:15): 'As a mother comforts her child, so will I comfort you' (Isaiah 66:13); but his Fatherhood stands out. And, thirdly, the Lord Jesus who is the Truth made it plain that it is the Father he reveals to us: 'All things have been committed to me by my Father. No one knows the Son except the Father, and no one knows the Father except the Son and those to whom the Son chooses to reveal him' (Matthew 11:27; cf. John 14:6-11). Desires to change this most eloquent description of God's relationship to his people spring either from a failure to understand the perfection of God's revelation in Scripture or from a preoccupation with sexist issues which tends to see threats everywhere.

THE ONLY GOD AND FATHER

The One of whom we speak, and to whom we address our prayers, is - to use the apostle Paul's words - the 'one God and Father of all, who is over all and through all and in all' (Ephesians 4:6). This statement may well have been part of an early Christian confession of faith. Although the world foolishly puts its trust in many gods, whether made with human hands in stone, wood, or metal, or in the contemporary world's seemingly more sophisticated gods of materialism, technology and sexual fulfilment, they are no gods at all. All created things and beings bear the mark of the same Creator, the Maker of heaven and earth. This Creator is the Father to whom we address our prayers. But Paul's words concerning the 'God and Father of all, who is over all and through all and in all' prompt a question.

WHOSE FATHER IS HE?

Scripture interprets Scripture, and comes to our aid here. Since to call God our Father is a benefit of faith in Jesus Christ, the implication is that God was not our Father before we believed.

So often people regard God as everyone's Father. But this is not the case. It is true that God has a kind of Fatherhood of all, in that he created everything and gives life and breath to all things (Acts 17:24-29; Hebrews 12:9; James 1:17; cf. John 8:44; Acts 13:10). But the Bible does not generally use the term 'Father' of God as Creator, but instead keeps it especially for those who have become his spiritual children through faith in his Son, Jesus Christ. Rather than being the Father of all, he is the Father of his own people, by an act of redemption. Writing to those 'in Christ' at Ephesus, Paul declared that the Father was 'in' them (Ephesians 4:6), something which is certainly not true of unbelievers. In the Old Testament as well as in the New, sonship springs from redemption (Exodus 4:22; Isaiah 1:2).

A FRUIT OF CALVARY

Of all the wonderful benefits that flow to Christian believers from the death of our Lord Jesus Christ, none surpasses this wonder of calling God 'Father'. Before our conversion, whether we understood it or not, we were cut off from him, and belonged to another family altogether - the evil one's family (John 8:41).

At our new birth God welcomed us into his family. He uses the two pictures of birth and adoption. Receiving his Son, we receive the right to become God's children, 'born not of natural descent, nor of human decision or a husband's will, but born of God' (John 1:13). God is the Father of those whom he delivers from this present evil age (Galatians 1:4), and whom he thus brings into living fellowship with himself and his Son by his Spirit's gracious indwelling. 'In love' God 'predestined us to be adopted as his sons' and daughters 'through Jesus Christ, in accordance with his pleasure and will' (Ephesians 1:4,5).

Adoption is even more wonderful than justification. In justification we are pronounced right with God the Judge; in adoption we are declared to be loved and cared for by God the Father as his children. Adoption was known as much in the ancient world as now. Under Roman law there was an elaborate procedure to undergo, but when complete, it was comprehensive in its effects. The person who had been adopted had all the rights of a legitimate son in his new family, and completely lost all rights in his old family. In the eyes of the law he was a new person. So new was he that even all debts and obligations connected with his previous family were cancelled as if they had never existed.

In justification, by God's sovereign act, we are declared righteous through the work of the Son of God, even though we know ourselves to be sinners. We are not made right in the sense of being made virtuous, but we are right with God. Through justification, we are as much at peace with God now as our Lord Jesus Christ! But in our adoption by God we are given the full rights and privileges of sonship in a family to which we do not belong by nature. Brought into such a wonderful relationship, we are day by day transformed into the likeness of God's dear Son, our Lord Jesus.

Significantly, Jesus did not include himself when he told the disciples to pray 'Our Father' since he is in a unique sense God's Son. Elsewhere he never associated himself with his disciples by using the personal pronoun 'our'. He always used the singular 'My Father'. He is the Son of God by nature; we become God's sons and daughters only by receiving him, and experiencing new birth (John 1:12) - a complete and utter miracle of God's grace.

CONTEMPORARY FATHERHOOD

The reality of human fatherhood is not known by all in our society, and, when it is, it may be tragically spoiled. An increasing number of children come from a single-parent family, and in the nature of things that means that most of them are without the experience of life with their own father. Sadly, child abuse is a feature of present day life, and responsibility for it rests often with the father of the family. The title 'Father', therefore, is not as appealing and as meaningful as it ought to be. We may sadly transfer unhappy feelings about our human father to God. Someone has described how she respected her father, but she was also a bit afraid of him. This latter aspect of the relationship was also part of his legacy to her. If her father said, 'Jump,' she would ask, 'How high?' She found she automatically transferred these feelings to God. We need to recapture the attractiveness of the name 'Father', and lift it above unhappy experiences and the tragedy of the abuse of human fatherhood.

THE FORGOTTEN FATHER

Christians too have been at fault in forgetting God's Fatherhood. The danger of new discoveries of truth or fresh emphases is the neglect of familiar truth. The charismatic movement - with its stress upon, and at times preoccupation with, the work of the Spirit - has sometimes been synonymous with a neglect of the other two Persons of the Trinity, and in particular God the Father. Prayer, for example, to the Lord Jesus may displace prayer to the Father. Now it cannot be wrong to pray to the Lord Jesus, for he is our Lord, and is the Second Person of the Trinity; but the Lord's Prayer teaches that the proper norm is to address prayer to the Father.

Thank God for every new awareness of his Spirit, and his work. But we must never forget that the anti-Christ denies the Father and the Son (1 John 2:22,23), and we must be cautious about anything that removes our focus from our Father and his Son.

THE PRIMARY FATHERHOOD

All fatherhood gets its meaning and inspiration from God's Fatherhood. Paul wrote, 'I kneel before the Father, from whom his whole family in heaven and on earth derives its name' (Ephesians 3:14,15). We do not call him 'Father' because features of his character remind us of our human parents. The opposite is the case: his is the true Fatherhood. His is not derived from ours; but ours from his. All we know of genuine human fatherhood at its best is but a pale reflection of what the Father is, first, to his Son, and then to all who become his spiritual children. It is because we are made in his image that we reflect that image in human fatherhood - and human motherhood. The name of father did not go up to God from us, it came down to us from God.

The Father is uniquely the Father, and there is no one else like him in Fatherhood (Matthew 23:9).

THE UNRIVALLED FATHERHOOD

God's Fatherhood of his spiritual children surpasses human fatherhood, and provides an example for all parents, since his is the perfect model. Human parents may love their children only when their children succeed, or may be influenced in their love by whether or not they are boys or girls. Our heavenly Father loves us whether we are successful or unsuccessful; male or female.

A Church of Scotland evangelist, Stephen Anderson, led a holiday mission among young people. He became aware that a team member lacked the peace and assurance which are part of our Christian birthright. He felt that he should say to her that 'her father only really loved her as a success whereas her Heavenly Father loved her for herself and just as she was.' This immediately went home. The girl, in floods of tears, 'spoke of how disappointed her father had been that she had been born a girl and had not entered the family business. The unconditional love of our Heavenly Father flooded over and into her to bring a new relief and unutterable joy.'

THE UNIQUE REVEALER OF THE FATHER

When God's people in the Old Testament period referred to God as Father (Isaiah 63:16), the title pointed to God's concern for the helpless, his care and discipline of his people (Proverbs 3:11,12; Isaiah 64:8), and their loyal reverential response to him (Jeremiah 3:4,19; Malachi 1:6). They knew him to be 'a father to the fatherless' (Psalm 68:5), and compassionate like a father (Psalm 103:13). But they did not enjoy the confidence of that relationship - not least in prayer. This awaited the coming of Jesus Christ, God's Son, the unique Revealer of the Father's nature and character.

We have never heard the Father's voice, but in Jesus God speaks to us. Jesus did not speak of his own accord, but he spoke only what the

Father commanded him to say, and how he should say it (John 12:49). To hear the Son is to hear the Father.

Every view we have of the Father, therefore, is to be totally influenced and guided by the life and teaching of the Lord Jesus. We have never seen the Father's form (John 5:37), for God is Spirit (John 4:24), but the Father has revealed himself in the Incarnation of his Son. To see the Son is to see the Father (John 12:45; 14:9). Jesus said to his critics, 'If you knew me, you would know my Father also' (John 8:19). When Philip requested, 'Lord, show us the Father and that will be enough for us,' Jesus answered, 'Don't you know me, Philip, even after I have been among you such a long time? Anyone who has seen me has seen the Father' (John 14:8,9). To look at Jesus is to see the One who sent him. All, therefore, who love the Father love the Son (John 8:42).

JESUS' REVELATION OF OUR FATHER'S CHARACTER

Jesus said much about the Father in his teaching. In the opening words of this prayer he says that **he is 'our Father in heaven'**. Fourteen times in the gospels he speaks of him like this (Matthew 5:16,45; 6:1,9; 7:11; 10:32,33; 12:50; 16:17; 18:10,14,19; Mark 11:25; Luke 11:13). Familiarity with the words, 'Our Father in heaven', could mean we pass over them too quickly and fail to see their importance. 'Our Father in heaven', may be a way of saying 'Our Divine Father' since 'heaven' was the word pious Jews substituted for the Divine Name. If so, we are saying, 'Our Father, you alone are God, the God of an Infinite Majesty.' As our heavenly Father, he is great. We should approach him with reverence.

While God is everywhere, in a special sense heaven is his dwelling place (Genesis 24:7; Deuteronomy 26:15; 1 Kings 8:30; 2 Chronicles 20:6; 30:27; Job 22:12; Psalm 73:25; 123:1; Isaiah 66:1; Jonah 1:9; Acts 7:49) in that there his glory is perfectly seen and acknowledged. The highest heaven, however, cannot contain him (1 Kings 8:27), and he may be said to fill heaven and earth (Jeremiah 23:24).

But the Lord Jesus taught much more about the Father. **Our Father is spirit** (John 4:24). He is not to be thought of in physical terms, and we are told not to make any image or picture of him (Exodus 20:4). Because of preoccupation with our physical bodies, we tend to think that the physical and material are essential to existence. They are not. As spirit, God is invisible and is not bound to places or things.

Our Father is all-powerful and sovereign. He has life in himself (John 5:26) and is always at work in the affairs of his creation (John 5:17). As the Almighty Lord, nothing is impossible to him (Mark 14:36). His control extends to the smallest details of life, so that not even a sparrow falls to the ground apart from his will (Matthew 10:29). To think of him properly is to think of his unbounded power and resources (Isaiah 6:5; 47:4). His sovereignty not only guarantees that history will end as he wills, but that he determines the outcome of all human activity according to his perfect righteousness. As John Calvin put it, 'The Lord will do what pleases him, his providence will see what is best. I have learnt by experience that we are not allowed to see too much of the future. ... If we trust in him, he will watch over us himself.' Whatever happens in the world, God is in his holy temple, available to his people (Psalm 11:4). When our lives are in his care, he sees to it that we lack nothing, and no good thing. (Psalm 34:9,10; Deuteronomy 6:24; Psalm 84:11; Romans 8:28). 'Our God is in the heavens; he does whatever pleases him' (Psalm 115:3).

Our Father is perfect. 'Be perfect ... as your heavenly Father is perfect,' Jesus instructed his disciples (Matthew 5:48). Nothing can be added to our Father. There can be no development in his character, for he is perfection. His sublime excellence is revealed in his attributes, all of which are in perfect harmony with one another. In him there is no excess, no defect, no inconsistency and no stain.

Our Father is good (Matthew 19:17; Mark 10:18; Luke 18:19; cf. Luke 11:13). It is not inappropriate to describe this as our Father's supreme characteristic. When we say that he is good we are declaring that he is all that he as God ought to be. He is good and always does good. 'How great is your goodness, which you have stored up for those who fear you, which you bestow in the sight of men on those who take refuge in you' (Psalm 31:19). He is so good that he makes all who trust in him truly happy in the deepest sense, so that they testify, 'Taste and see that the LORD is good; blessed is the man who takes refuge in him' (Psalm 34:8).

Our Father is holy. 'Holy Father,' is how our Lord Jesus addressed his Father (John 17:11). His holiness is his total and unique moral majesty. Because we are unlike him by reason of our sinfulness, his holiness is the attribute we are most aware of when we begin to seek after him. It is so great that it can be expressed only by a super-superlative: 'Holy, holy, holy is the LORD Almighty' (Isaiah 6:3; Revelation 4:8). Linked with our Father's holiness is **his glory**, for his glory is his awesome holiness. The glory the Lord Jesus revealed, which made Peter call out, 'Go away from me, Lord; I am a sinful man!' (Luke 5:8), was the Father's glory, and when our Saviour returns he will come in that same glory (Matthew 16:27).

Our Father is righteous (John 17:25) **and just** (Matthew 18:35). His righteousness is his holiness expressed in moral principles, and his justice is the application of those righteous principles. Our heavenly Father always acts in accordance with what is right. To act rightly is essential to his nature. When law and order collapse, and men and women abandon what is right, the foundations of his righteousness remain (Psalm 11:3-7). This is a reality upon which to depend in an unrighteous and unjust world. In a hymn entitled 'The Right Must Win', Faber writes,

> *God's justice is a bed, where we*
> *Our anxious hearts may lay,*
> *And, weary with ourselves, may sleep*
> *Our discontent away.*
>
> *For right is right, since God is God;*
> *And right the day must win;*
> *To doubt would be disloyalty,*
> *To falter would be sin.*

Our Father is merciful (Luke 6:36), **loving** (John 3:16), **forgiving** (Matthew 6:14) and **generous** (Matthew 7:11; Luke 11:13). These aspects of his character unite in perfect harmony in the story Jesus told of the reception a father gave to his returning son (Luke 15:20-24). 'Be merciful, just as your Father is merciful,' Jesus commands us (Luke 6:36). Our Father's mercy is his warm affection towards the needy, helpless and distressed. While the prodigal son 'was still a long way off, his father saw him and was filled with compassion for him' (Luke 15:20). God has shown his amazing mercy in sending his Son to be our Saviour (Luke 1:78; Titus 3:5).

In the New Testament **the Father's love** is singled out as the special characteristic of his dealings with us as his children in Christ (John 3:16; 16:27; Romans 5:5; 2 Corinthians 13:14; Titus 3:4; 1 John 4:8). The more we turn over the truth of his Fatherhood and its loving character, the more we know and feel we can trust him for everything and in everything.

Someone told me about a lesson his son taught him. His son went up to university. It was his first time away from home, and the father was somewhat apprehensive for his son. His concern was increased when they arrived at the university hall of residence. The room was but a little box, and the noise from adjacent rooms was loud. As he went out of the hall of residence, he slipped a fairly substantial sum of money into the hand of the janitor, saying quietly to him, 'Keep a good eye on my boy, please.'

As they came away from the hall of residence, the son said to his father, 'What did you give to the janitor just then, and what did you say to him?' The father admitted what he had done and said. The son looked at his father and said, 'Dad, remember you are my **human** father, but I also have a **heavenly** Father who will look after me.' The father felt rebuked, and realised that his trust needed to be in that Father as his son's clearly was.

God's love is greater than all our natural parents' love at its best. Alfred Bosshardt was leaving home for missionary service in China. He wrote to his family telling them how he had been thinking and picturing them. 'Yesterday as I prayed and thanked the Lord for the love of an earthly father, I felt the arms of my Heavenly Father around me.' 'Though my father and mother forsake me, the LORD will receive me,'

David wrote (Psalm 27:10). The one picture we have of God in a hurry is in the story of the prodigal when the father runs out to embrace his repentant son. God's love now is the love he showed when he gave his Son to die for us upon the Cross. To rest our souls in his love is their true rest. From our Father's mercy and love flow his perfect pardon of our sins. There is no greater proof of love than the exercise of forgiveness. Our Father's mercy, love and forgiveness are unimaginably generous.

REASSURING TRUTHS ABOUT GOD'S FATHERHOOD

The Lord Jesus spoke especially about the Father's character in relation to his spiritual children. First, **our Father knows our needs**. For him to know is for him to act on our behalf. For God to see the need of his people is synonymous with his taking action for their good. Seeing the need of his people in captivity in Egypt, he came down to rescue them (Exodus 3:7,8; cf. Psalm 102:19,20). Urging us not to worry about how long we shall live, and the provision of food and housing, Jesus says, 'For the pagans run after all these things, and your heavenly Father knows that you need them' (Matthew 6:32).

Our Father's perfect knowledge has practical consequences for his family: we are always in his sight, and he knows exactly what we need, even better than we do. Knowing the future as perfectly as he knows the past and present, he anticipates our needs. Nothing in our circumstances takes him by surprise. In sharing our concerns and worries with him in prayer, we do not give him knowledge of our need, but rather we respond to his complete knowledge of us. When we cry to him for help it is an unending comfort to know he is aware of all our needs.

Secondly, **our Father delights to give good gifts to his children**. 'Ask and it will be given to you; seek and you will find; knock and the door will be opened to you. For everyone who asks receives; he who seeks finds; and to him who knocks, the door will be opened' (Matthew 7:7,8). Our Lord then asks a question and from the inevitable answer he draws a telling lesson: 'Which of you, if his son asks for bread, will give him a stone? Or if he asks for a fish, will give him a snake? If you, then, though you are evil, know how to give good gifts to your children, how much more will your Father in heaven give good gifts to those who ask him!' (Matthew 7:9-11). In the familiar words of James 1:5, where he writes of God giving his wisdom to us generously, James' actual words are that our Father is 'the giving God'!

So great is our Father's delight in giving, we are encouraged to use the 'how much more' argument. Since all true fatherhood reflects God's image in us, we are to argue, 'If something is true of human fatherhood at its best, it is even more the case with our Heavenly Father!' Chief Jongintaba Dalindyebo was the acting regent of the Themba people in South Africa. When Nelson Mandela's father died, he offered to become Nelson's guardian and to be as a father to him. Nelson Mandela wrote, 'I always knew, even when I was estranged from the regent, that all my friends might desert me, all my plans might founder, all my hopes be dashed, but the regent would never abandon me.' If that can be said of someone who acts as a father to us, how much more can it be said of God the true and perfect Father!

Thirdly, **our Father makes - or gives - promises for our encouragement** - promises upon which we may utterly depend. He is 'God, who does not lie' (Titus 1:2). His promises are food for our faith. He promises his kingdom, which he prepares for us, when we shall share in our Saviour's glory: 'Do not be afraid, little flock,' Jesus says, 'for your Father has been pleased to give you the kingdom' (Luke 12:32; cf. Matthew 25:34). He promises us his Spirit, and power to live to please God (Luke 24:49). Our Father's fondness for us goes far beyond our wildest dreams. He assures us of his fatherly love to win our confidence.

THE KEY WORD

'Father' is prayer's key word. In most languages it signifies nourisher, protector and upholder. No name surpasses its significance and power. Two women arrived as Bible translators in a village in the Philippines. One of them, Joanne Shetler, has described how Canao, the village's spokesman, came to them after they had been there a few days 'without a trace of his usual smile. He was outwardly calm' but they could 'feel his tension and heard it in his voice.' '"Don't you realise it's not safe for women to be here? Don't you know we're headhunters?" He let that sink in and then, with a sigh, said, "You need someone to take care of you - I'll be your father!" He gave a short, deliberate nod, sealing his words with final authority.'

The name 'Father' reminds us of to whom it is that we are privileged to address our prayers. While it is not inappropriate to pray to the Son and the Holy Spirit, the Bible teaches that it is through the Son that we 'have access to the Father by one Spirit' (Ephesians 2:18). In the Lord Jesus and through faith in him we may approach the Father with freedom and without fear (Ephesians 3:12). Our Saviour told his disciples that they were to ask the Father for what they needed rather than pray to him: 'In that day you will no longer ask me anything. I tell you the truth, my Father will give you whatever you ask in my name' (John 16:23).

The Christian life is a relationship with God the Father through Jesus Christ, his Son, by the power of God's Spirit. Vital to living that life is our understanding and appreciating God's Fatherhood. He calls himself our Father, and he wants us to depend upon him as such. Satan, the enemy of our souls, constantly tries to rob us of this assurance. Think again of the prodigal son. Looking at himself and the mess he had made of his life, he begged his father to make him like one of his hired servants (Luke 15:19). To do that was beyond the realms of possibility with such a glorious father! And so it is with our Father!

So important is this name 'Father' and the relationship it indicates, God's immediate act upon our new birth is to put into our lips the cry, 'Abba, Father' (Romans 8:15). 'Abba' is an Aramaic word meaning, 'Father'. (Aramaic is a Semitic language, closely related to Hebrew, which our Lord Jesus spoke.) It is the familiar term a child would use in the home of its father, spoken with reverence, so that our English equivalent would not be so much 'Daddy' but rather 'Dear Father'. Adopted into the family circle of God, we can say with a full heart, 'Father, my Father'. God's Spirit tells us deep within our hearts that we really are God's children (Romans 8:16). This is the Spirit's unique and special work. John Wesley described how the crisis of his own assurance of salvation came when, in his own words, he 'exchanged the faith of a servant for the faith of a son'.

Martin Luther, the sixteenth century reformer, particularly appreciated the word 'Father'. He said, 'This is indeed a very short word, but it includes everything. Not the lips, but the feelings are speaking here, as though one were to say: Even though I am surrounded by anxieties and seem to be deserted and banished from your presence, nevertheless I am a child of God on account of Christ; I am beloved on account of the Beloved! Therefore the term "Father" when spoken meaningfully in the heart, is an eloquence ... the most eloquent of men there have been in the world cannot attain. For this is a matter that is expressed, not in words but in sighs, which are not articulated in all the words of all the orators; for they are too deep for words' (Luther on Galatians 4:6). Thomas Chalmers was a prominent evangelical minister in nineteenth century Scotland. The night before his death, he walked in his gardens behind his house and he 'was overheard by one of his family in low but very earnest tones, saying, "O Father, my heavenly Father!"'

Nothing increases our confidence to pray more than appreciating that God is our Father, especially when we grasp afresh his unspeakable love behind our adoption! He wants to bless us because he loves us as his sons and daughters. The love he has for us - because we are 'in Christ' - is the love he has for his only begotten Son!

CONSEQUENCES

Privilege brings responsibility; and our relationship to our Father does. We are to follow his example in everything (Ephesians 5:1): we are to aim to be like him in his kindness (Matthew 5:44,45), and forgiveness (Mark 11:25; Luke 23:34). We are to trust him in all circumstances, and to be submissive to him (Mark 14:36; Luke 22:42; 23:46). We are to receive his correction gratefully, recognising that it is always for our good (Hebrews 12:5-13).

We are to remember too our relationship with others who likewise call him 'Father' by the same indwelling Spirit. We are taught to say '**Our** Father'. This prayer belongs neither to me alone nor to any particular group of Christians. It belongs to all who have been born and adopted into God's family. My new birth not only enables me to call God 'Father' but it gives me countless brothers and sisters. The whole family of the redeemed are under the one Father who is the Father of our Lord Jesus Christ (Ephesians 3:14,15). Picture putting together a converted Scot and a converted Bornean tribesman in an international conference. One may have been brought up in the best of schools and universities, and in a seemingly advanced culture. The other may have had little formal education, in a totally different cultural environment. And yet in half an hour they will feel that they are friends and - better still - brothers. They will know that they have more important things in common with one another than with their unbelieving compatriots. The explanation is God's Spirit indwelling each as sons of God.

When we pray 'Our Father in heaven' we are called upon to think of our brothers and sisters on earth. To pray this prayer puts us in fellowship with them. We are to mirror our Father's character in our relationships with one another (e.g. Numbers 11:12; cf. Deuteronomy 1:31; Matthew 18:35). Calling him 'Father', we are to behave as his sons and daughters. We please our Father as we care about his family. Human families naturally care about the family name and reputation. Members of God's family not only care about the family name, but - more important still - they care about the Father's Name, and the reputation of his Son in that family. That is where the next part of the Lord's Prayer will take us.

THE UPWARD LOOK

We may sometimes pray and feel at the end that we have not really prayed. A variety of reasons may be the cause. But an important lesson is taught us here: we should start with the upward look (Matthew 14:19; Mark 6:41; 7:34; Luke 9:16) All prayer needs to begin with the confidence of our wonderfully intimate relationship to God through his Son Jesus Christ.

As we look up to God, coming in his Son's Name, asking for his Spirit's assistance, we see God first as our Father. With our eyes on him, we rejoice afresh that we are his children! Basking in his fatherly love, we then find no difficulty in pouring out our hearts to him. Just as we cannot light a fire by a mirror without first pointing it to the sun, so we cannot light the fire of prayer in our heart without first turning our eyes to our Father.

As we look up, guided by our Saviour's words, we see him, secondly, as 'Our Father **in heaven**'. Heaven is the unique vantage point from which everything on earth is seen: 'From heaven the LORD looks down and sees all mankind, from his dwelling-place he watches all who live on earth' (Psalm 33:13,14; cf. 53:2; 102:19). It is from heaven our Father speaks (Genesis 21:17; 22:11,15; Exodus 20:22; Nehemiah 9:13; Matthew 3:17), sends his help (Psalm 57:3) and his blessings come (Malachi 3:10).

Go in your imagination to the Houses of Parliament, the seat of government in the United Kingdom, or to the White House, the official residence of the President of the United States of America - places where the world imagines authority to be - and then lift up your eyes to your Father, and say, 'Our Father in heaven'. All authority and power are his. With him as our Father we have every encouragement to pray!

RIGHT VIEWS OF GOD

Before our new birth we almost certainly had many wrong views of God, sown in our minds by Satan. But as God shines into our hearts showing us his glory in the face of Jesus Christ, we see what God is truly like, and how utterly trustworthy he is (2 Corinthians 4:6). Seeing the Son, we see the Father (John 14:8,9). Every view we have of God's character is to be totally influenced by what we see in our Lord Jesus Christ, the perfect image of the Father.

God's Fatherhood is the proper starting point in all our happiness and joys since he shares them with us. Glad at the way the disciples undertook a preaching mission with the good news of the gospel, and the success that attended their efforts, our Lord Jesus' first response 'full of joy through the Holy Spirit' was to say, 'I praise you, Father, Lord of heaven and earth, because you have hidden these things from the wise and learned, and have revealed them to little children' (Luke

10:21). Filled too with God's Spirit, our first response in every occasion of joy will be to praise and thank our Father. As his children, the outworking of our Father's will in Christ Jesus is for us to be joyful always, to pray continually, and to give thanks in all circumstances (1 Thessalonians 5:16-18).

God's Fatherhood must also be our starting point in sorrows and trials. Thankfully, life holds many joys for most of us, but inevitably sorrows and trials figure at some stage. In the Garden of Gethsemane, with the sufferings of the Cross before him, our Lord's prayer of obedient submission was prefaced by the word 'Father': '**Father**, if you are willing, take this cup from me; yet not my will, but yours be done' (Luke 22:42). His last words on the Cross likewise were, '**Father**, into your hands I commit my spirit' (Luke 23:46).

TRUSTING CHILDREN

Trusting children is the first picture the Lord's Prayer provides of what it means to be a Christian. That is entirely appropriate since one of the first acts of a man or woman born into God's family is to cry 'Father'. We are trusting children because of our Father's character. Trust always hinges upon perception of a person's integrity. We trust someone when we are sure of him or her. Nothing must rob us of the simplicity, yet depth, of our relationship to God as his children. We have a speaking relationship to God. The key to dealing with every challenge to faith and all our problems is to look first to him.

Chapter 2

Reverent worshippers

'Hallowed be your name'

T hat this is the first petition in the Lord's Prayer points to its importance. It comes first to show that the hallowing of God's Name is to be our great priority in life. Our two concerns are to understand the emphasis upon his 'Name' and what is meant by hallowing it.

A GENERAL WESTERN NEGLECT

In the west we do not place great importance upon a person's name. It is very much a matter of convenience. It provides a means of establishing someone's identity rather than telling us anything about a person's character. If a name has famous connections, we might then be inclined to take more notice.

The family name of Guinness is very well known in the Republic of Ireland. Michelle Guinness tells of how she was in Dublin to speak at a Women's Luncheon Club, when the strap of her sandal snapped. She went into the first shoe repair shop she could find. 'Could you do them now, this minute?' she pleaded. The assistant shook her head slowly, unmoved by her predicament. 'There's a long waiting list. Sure, you'll have to wait your turn, and it'll take two days.' 'But it only needs a stitch.' There was no response and she would have left the shop there and then, were it not for the fact that it is impossible to go anywhere wearing only one shoe. 'Name?' the shop assistant asked. 'Guinness,' she responded. There was a moment's silence. Then without looking up the assistant said, 'Your shoes will be ready in five minutes, Mrs. Guinness.' Such is the power of a name which is well known and well connected. But the Bible's emphasis on the name has more behind it than this.

We get nearer to its biblical significance in Africa. An American living among the Masai in Tanzania saw nothing wrong, according to his own culture, in telling them his name and asking theirs. He was advised, however, that the Masai regarded this as very rude. In public and with strangers they used titles or designations, not names. One day a Masai man said to him: 'Do not throw my name about. My name is important. My name is me. My name is for my friends.' In the Bible God's Name stands for all he has revealed about himself - his being and attributes. His Name is especially for his friends. Revelation is essentially the disclosure of God's Name.

THE SIGNIFICANCE OF GOD'S NAME

'You have exalted above all things your name and your word,' David declares to God (Psalm 138:2). Here God's Name comes first, as in the Lord's Prayer. God's Name and Word go together, because it is by what he says to us - his Word - that he tells us his Name.

God appeared to Moses in the burning bush to call him to serve his people. Moses asked what he should answer when the Israelites inquired about the name of the God who had sent him. 'God said to Moses, "I AM WHO I AM. This is what you are to say to the Israelites: 'I AM has sent me to you' " ' (Exodus 3:14). What made Moses so privileged was that God proclaimed his Name - the LORD - in his presence. 'Moses said, "Now show me your glory." And the LORD said, "I will cause all my goodness to pass in front of you, and I will proclaim my name, the LORD, in your presence. I will have mercy on whom I will have mercy, and I will have compassion on whom I will have compassion' (Exodus 33:18,19).

God's Name signifies God himself: it stands for God's revealed character, his essence, his attributes (Exodus 34:5-7). The Book of Psalms, for instance, describes God's Name as majestic (Psalm 8:1,9), good (Psalm 52:9), loving (Psalm 115:1), faithful (Psalm 115:1), trustworthy (Psalm 9:10), and enduring (Psalm 135:13). God is all of these things and more. 'Who is like you,' we may ask, as did Moses and the Israelites, 'majestic in holiness, awesome in glory, working wonders?' (Exodus 15:11).

THE REVELATION OF GOD'S NAME IN CREATION

God has revealed his Name in creation. 'The heavens declare the glory of God; the skies proclaim the work of his hands. Day after day they pour forth speech; night after night they display knowledge. There is no speech or language where their voice is not heard. Their voice goes out into all the earth, their words to the ends of the world' (Psalm 19:1-4). No man or woman who looks intelligently at the created world can fail to see evidences not only of a Creator but also of his character. 'For since the creation of the world, God's invisible qualities - his eternal power and divine nature - have been clearly seen, being understood from what has been made, so that men are without excuse' (Romans 1:20). Creation's voice proclaims God's Name or character. Even as everything we make bears the imprint of our personality, so God's created works bear the stamp of his character. So David declared, 'I praise you because I am fearfully and wonderfully made; your works are wonderful, I know that full well' (Psalm 139:14). In all that God has created, including ourselves, his nature is revealed.

GOD'S REVELATION OF HIS NAME TO HIS PEOPLE

God makes himself known in the Bible chiefly by means of his Names, glorious titles which set before us his perfection. God revealed his Name to the Jews, his chosen people. To Abraham, Isaac and Jacob, he revealed himself as El Shaddai - 'I am God Almighty' (Genesis 17:1; 35:11).

Two names predominate in the Old Testament: **Elohim,** the Creator and Universal Ruler, and **Jehovah,** or **Yahweh,** the redeeming and covenant God. At the burning bush God revealed himself as the God of the patriarchs - **Elohim,** the superhuman and supernatural One (Exodus 3:6). **Elohim** comes from **alah** 'to be in fear of' and reminds us that the Almighty God is to be held in reverence. The name is strengthened by the plural ending **im,** the plural of Divine fulness, although the verb always remains in the singular, clearly expressing the Divine unity and plurality.

Foremost in God's disclosure of his Name was his revelation to Moses at the burning bush: 'I AM WHO I AM' (Exodus 3:14). We cannot be dogmatic as to how God's Name was pronounced. The vowels were forgotten in a time when the Name was thought to be too holy to be spoken aloud. It seems that the pronunciation was 'Yahweh' or something like it. The form **Yahweh** represents the consonants of **Yahweh** (Jahweh) combined with the vowels of another word (**Adonai**) which was substituted for **Yahweh** in the public reading of the Hebrew Bible, to avoid using the holier name. In the English translation of the Old Testament 'Lord' always begins with a capital letter, and three times out of four it is printed 'LORD'. 'Lord' - not printed in capitals - represents **Adonai**, literally 'my lord', a regular title for God derived from the Hebrew **adon** which means master or governor. 'LORD' - in capitals - represents Jehovah or Yahweh.

'I AM' bears the sense of 'what I will be, I will be.' God's Name proclaims his sovereignty, his self-sufficiency and self-consistency: he does what he wills; he acts as he pleases, and always in a way consistent with his absolute goodness. His Name I AM points to the perfection and eternity of his being. What he has always possessed, he now possesses; and what he has now, he will always have. With him, there is neither beginning nor end. What he promises he fulfils; and he is the God of limitless life and power.

His Name 'I AM' underlines the reality of his being in opposition to idols and other so-called gods: 'We know that an idol is nothing at all in the world and that there is no God but one. For even if there are so-called gods, whether in heaven or on earth (as indeed there are many "gods" and many "lords"), yet for us there is but one God, the Father, from whom all things came and for whom we live' (1 Corinthians 8:4-6).

No words - no names - are capable of expressing perfectly what God is. There is a sense, therefore, in which his Name is secret. The conception and birth of Samson were promised to Manoah and his wife by the angel of the Lord. (The angel of the Lord was what we call a 'theophany' - a pre-incarnation appearance of God the Son, our Lord Jesus Christ.) When Manoah asked the angel of the Lord, 'What is your name, so that we may honour you when your word comes true?' the answer he received was significant. 'He replied, "Why do you ask my name? It is beyond understanding"' (Judges 13:17,18). 'Beyond understanding' means wonderful, separate from everything else, surpassing and inexpressible. Proverbs 30:4 conveys the sense of wonder that is appropriate when we consider God's Name: 'Who has gone up to heaven and come down? Who has gathered up the wind in the hollow of his hands? Who has wrapped up the waters in his cloak? Who has established all the ends of the earth? What is his name, and the name of his son? Tell me if you know!'

There are also particular names of God arising often out of special incidents and circumstances, such as -

Jehovah-Jireh, 'The LORD will provide' (Genesis 22:14);

Jehovah-Ropheka, 'The LORD, who heals you' (Exodus 15:26);

Jehovah-Nissi: 'The LORD is my Banner' (Exodus 17:15);

Jehovah-Shalom: 'The LORD is peace' (Judges 6:24);

Jehovah-Sabaoth: 'The LORD Almighty' (1 Samuel 1:3);

Jehovah-Rohi: 'The LORD is my Shepherd' (Psalm 23:1);

Jehovah-Zidkenu: 'The LORD Our Righteousness' (Jeremiah 23:6);

Jehovah-Shammah: 'The LORD IS THERE' (Ezekiel 48:35).

The names of God are important for our knowledge of him. Hudson Taylor, a missionary pioneer in China, discovered this truth when for a whole month he was confined to his bed, and he found time to meditate. He began to paint on scrolls in Chinese characters two Hebrew place-names which the Old Testament records and explains: **Eben-ezer** and **Jehovah-jireh**. He read in 1 Samuel 7 how after Israel had been given a great victory in answer to prayer, Samuel took a stone, and named it **Ebenezer**, saying, 'Thus far has the LORD helped us' (1 Samuel 7:12). He also read in Genesis 22 that when the Lord prevented Abraham from sacrificing Isaac and provided instead a ram, Abraham called that place **Jehovah-jireh**, 'The LORD will provide' (Genesis 22:14). Whenever Hudson Taylor was tempted to doubt or to be anxious, he looked again at the words on his scrolls. 'My faith,' he wrote, 'often, often failed, and I was so sorry and ashamed of my failure to trust such a Father. But oh! I was learning to know him ... He became so real and intimate.' Hudson Taylor would have agreed with the words of Augustus Toplady,

When we in darkness walk,
Nor feel the heavenly flame,
Then is the time to trust our God,
And rest upon his Name.

THE REVELATION OF GOD'S NAME IN HIS LAW

God has further revealed his Name in his law, which is a written and exact disclosure of his will. As his will expresses his nature (i.e. his Name), so his law expresses his will for us in a direct, comprehensive and memorable form. When God's law declares, 'Be holy, because I am holy' (Leviticus 11:45; cf. 19:2; 20:7; 1 Peter 1:16), it proclaims the priority of his Name, his holy character. The Divine nature expresses itself in the Divine law, the formal expression of his everlasting and universal authority.

THE FINAL REVELATION OF GOD'S NAME IN HIS SON

Our Lord Jesus, who is the Word - the One through whom God uniquely speaks - revealed the Father's Name, the Father's character. He did this first by what he said, so that, for example, he proclaimed God's Name as 'Father', as he does in this prayer. He did so, secondly, by his life and character, for his grace and truth show us the Father's glory (John 1:14). In the Lord Jesus all of God's Name - its full content - came to live among us. Praying to his Father, the Lord Jesus declared, 'I have made you known to them' - literally, 'I have made known your Name to them' (John 17:26). He could say, 'Anyone who has seen me has seen the Father' (John 14:9).

GOD'S PEOPLE'S UNIQUE PRIVILEGE

Some regiments in the British army are special because Her Majesty the Queen has given her name to them, and they are known by her name.

Famous regiments, for instance, have been The Queen's Regiment and The Queen's Own Cameron Highlanders. In addition, there have been other regiments to which the title 'Royal' has been attached, like The Royal Scots Dragoon Guards, and so on. They are marked out, and distinguished from, other parts of the Army because of this privilege.

God's people are special because he puts his Name upon them, in order to declare his relationship to them - a relationship which brings safety, grace and peace (Numbers 6:24-27). We are uniquely privileged to know his Name and to be called by it (2 Chronicles 7:14; cf. Isaiah 63:19) - an expression of the intimate union of God with his people.

HONOURING GOD AS HOLY

To hallow God's Name is to honour him as holy. The angels in heaven single out his holiness in their worship, declaring, 'Holy, holy, holy is the LORD Almighty; the whole earth is full of his glory' (Isaiah 6:3). The adjective 'holy' is put with God's Name in the Old Testament more frequently than all other adjectives put together. God's glory is his holiness; it is the very heart of his nature, his moral perfection. Holiness is the beauty and glory of God's other attributes. His greatness is especially seen in his holiness (Isaiah 12:6).

Holiness is God's foremost attribute when men and women encounter God. The prophet Isaiah was given a special revelation of God's character (Isaiah 6:1-3) and the aspect of God's being that came home to him most was his holiness. Significantly Isaiah is known as the prophet of holiness. He uses the adjective 'holy' of God more frequently than all the rest of the Old Testament. Such is the effect of an understanding of God's Name.

To hallow God's Name is to stand in awe of him (Isaiah 29:23; Malachi 2:5). It is significant that in one breath we use words of familiarity - 'our Father' - and in the next we utter words of reverence - 'Hallowed be your Name'. There is no contradiction. Our Lord Jesus himself addressed his Father as 'Holy Father' (John 17:11), and submitted himself to the Father with reverent obedience (Hebrews 5:7). Our delight in bold access to our Father is not inconsistent with deep respect. Becoming God's children takes away our terror of God, but not our reverence for him. Ours is not the fear we might associate with employees uncertain of their employer's character, but the reverence and awe of members of God's family (Hebrews 12:28).

THE VITAL PLACE OF PERSONAL HOLINESS

John Bunyan, author of the Christian classic *The Pilgrim's Progress,* wrote a book in 1684 significantly entitled, *A Holy Life: the Beauty of Christianity.* The New Testament never appeals for holiness in terms of law. Rather it appeals to our reason: nothing is more reasonable than that we should reflect our heavenly Father's character. If we claim to be the Father's children it makes sense that we should live as such. By holiness we show that we are children of our heavenly Father. As Thomas Watson, the Puritan, put it, 'When our lives shine, his Name shines in us.' We hallow God's Name as we strive after personal holiness.

THE PLACE TO BEGIN IS OUR HEART AND OUR RESPONSE TO HIS WORD

To hallow God's Name is to adore and respect him in our hearts, and to delight in his Word. God's complaint against those who profess to be his people but who dishonour him is, 'These people honour me with their lips, but their hearts are far from me' (Matthew 15:8). There is something of the hypocrite in us all. The word 'hypocrite' - a word of Greek origin - originally meant someone who answered or interpreted, but it came to mean an actor or someone who played a part. Hypocrites are not always deliberate actors, but if we are not careful we can play a part in public which is not genuinely true of us in private. To perform outward acts is so much easier than cultivating inner attitudes.

Sincerity and truth are what God requires (Psalm 51:6). He looks for reverence that is spiritual and genuine (John 4:23,24). It is in the intimacy of our hearts that God desires that we should acknowledge and worship him, by having high and holy thoughts about him. Wisely the writer of Proverbs urges, 'Above all else, guard your heart, for it is the wellspring of life' (Proverbs 4:23). The heart is the centre or core of our inner life; it is there that the direction of our life is determined and our basic commitments decided.

Our Lord Jesus taught that the Father and he delight to make their home with obedient believers: 'If anyone loves me, he will obey my teaching. My Father will love him, and we will come to him and make our home with him' (John 14:23). This makes sense since God has exalted above everything his Name and his Word (Psalm 138:2). We ourselves cannot be separated from our words. Others get to know us by what we say, as well as by what we do. In the same way we cannot separate God from his Word, the Bible. To honour his Name in our hearts, therefore, is to make obedience our deliberate practice every time we hear or read his Word. David, who has the distinction of being known as a man after God's own heart, hid God's Word in his heart, so that he might not sin against him (Psalm 119:11). When we receive God's Word as we ought, we honour it, and in honouring it, we honour God (Acts 13:48; 2 Thessalonians 3:1).

AN ILLUSTRATION

A most powerful illustration of the priority of obedience in our hallowing of God's Name is the sad example of Moses' and Aaron's failure at Kadesh (Numbers 20:1-13); it is one of those unhappy incidents recorded as a warning (1 Corinthians 10:11). When the time of Moses' death was close, he climbed Mount Nebo to view the promised land from a distance. God reminded Moses that the reason why both he and Aaron had forfeited the privilege of entering Canaan was that 'you did not uphold my holiness' - literally 'hallow me' (Deuteronomy 32:51). The reference is to what happened at Meribah-Kadesh. There 'the LORD became angry' with Moses (Deuteronomy 1:37; 3:26; 4:21).

We need to compare carefully God's precise instructions to Moses and the manner in which he executed them, for it was at this point he was disobedient and failed to hallow God's Name. Desperate for water,

Moses and Aaron sought God's help, 'and the glory of the LORD appeared to them. The LORD said to Moses, "Take the staff, and you and your brother Aaron gather the assembly together. Speak to that rock before their eyes and it will pour out its water. You will bring water out of the rock for the community so that they and their livestock can drink"' (Numbers 20:6-8). It is possible that the rock was a symbol of God's presence for he is frequently described as his people's Rock. But whatever may be the case, the particular mistake of Moses and Aaron was in their failure to obey precisely what God said.

God's instruction was that they were to 'speak to that rock' in order that it might produce water. But instead Moses spoke to the people, and **then** he struck the rock, **not just once, but twice**. The narrative reads, 'So Moses took the staff from the LORD's presence, just as he commanded him' (Numbers 20:9). Thus far was right. But then the record goes on, 'He and Aaron gathered the assembly together in front of the rock and Moses said to them, "Listen, you rebels, must we bring you water out of this rock?"' (Numbers 20:10). Notice the word 'we'. Rather than drawing attention to God's action, Moses drew attention to his own dramatic action, and his implied personal power. Moses went beyond what God had commanded, and in doing so he drew attention to himself rather than exalting God. He did not obey God's bare word; he felt he had to do more than God said - which is unbelief. We do not hallow God's Name when we disobey him or fail to believe what he says. Probably the Israelites who observed Moses' action saw no reason to fault him - for certainly his actions were effective in bringing forth water from the rock. But God searches the heart, and he discerned Moses' and Aaron's disobedience and unbelief. Obedience to God in our heart is personal, known only to him and to us. But unless we obey him there, we will not hallow his Name by the way we live (cf. 1 Peter 3:15).

THE CARE WE NEED TO EXERCISE IN OUR WORDS

To hallow God's Name is to show respect and reverence in the manner in which we speak about him. We must take into account Exodus 20:7:

'You shall not misuse the name of the LORD your God, for the LORD will not hold anyone guiltless who misuses his name.' It is 'out of the overflow of the heart the mouth speaks' (Matthew 12:34; Luke 6:45), and that is why we began with our hearts. Our tongue is the most powerful part of our body, because it can do both tremendous good and horrific damage. We sin with our words more than in any other way. 'If anyone is never at fault in what he says, he is a perfect man, able to keep his whole body in check' (James 3:2). Isaiah's immediate reaction on glimpsing God's holiness was to confess that he was a man of unclean lips (Isaiah 6:5).

We use words to speak of God's character (Psalm 69:30; 145:1ff). We need to be thoughtful and wise in how we speak of him. We hallow his Name every time we speak about him in accord with his self-revelation in his Word and in his Son. For example, it is not enough to say 'God is love', without saying also that 'God is light.' But we must not proclaim him as light without also declaring his love. We occasionally may have cause to use God's Name in oaths and vows. We hallow his Name by deeply respecting the solemnity of any such requirement. 'Do not swear falsely by my name and so profane the name of your God. I am the LORD,' He says to us (Leviticus 19:12).

We may sometimes be tempted to use God's Name to impress others. Jacob provides an unhappy example. Isaac, in his old age, was about to impart his blessing upon his sons. But first he asked Esau to go and hunt some wild game for him to eat. Rachel, Jacob's mother, was determined that he should receive his father's blessing in preference to Esau, his older twin brother. Because of Isaac's blindness, she encouraged Jacob to deceive his father by impersonating Esau, and in particular by covering his hands and the smooth part of his neck with goatskins to make him resemble his somewhat hairy brother. When Jacob, so disguised, presented food from the family's goat flock instead of wild game, Isaac asked, 'How did you find it so quickly my son?' Jacob replied, 'The LORD your God gave me success' (Genesis 27:20). To deceive his father was bad enough, but to use God's Name in such a way increased his sin.

We must beware of lightly introducing God's Name into our conversation. In the Old Testament false prophets gave their message and then said it was the Lord who had spoken to them and sent them (Jeremiah 23:25; 29:9). Sir David Frost describes an incident in his biography which illustrates this danger. He was interviewing Leland Hayward who negotiated the rights for the film 'The Sound of Music', based upon the life of Baroness von Trapp. In an interview Leland Hayward told of his visit to her in order to get her permission to be portrayed in the film. He sought to be as generous as possible, and said, '"We are portraying you in the best possible way ... but we do need your permission, of course, and I am prepared to make a very generous suggestion to you of ten per cent of the profits. **Ten per cent** of the profits." Leland had expected an immediate, pleasantly surprised and deeply grateful acceptance. Instead the Baroness replied, "My dear Mr. Hayward. I never make any decision like this without the help of the Holy Ghost, so if you will excuse me for a moment, I will go to the church to consult the Holy Ghost." She rose, gathered up her live-in priest and went off to church, leaving Leland and his wife sitting there for an hour. The Baroness finally returned, smiled a beatific smile, and said, "My dear Mr. Hayward, the Holy Ghost says fifteen per cent."' Are we not in danger sometimes of saying, 'The Lord told me' or 'The Lord led me', when it is sheer presumption and wishful thinking to say so? And is not his Name dishonoured when events prove that he neither told us nor led us in the direction we claimed? Even if we believe God has graciously confirmed his will to us, it may not be wise to state dogmatically to others that he has done so - for we are always fallible in our apprehension of his will.

We sometimes use God's Name to justify our actions. That may be right, as, for example, when Peter and John defended their preaching of the Lord Jesus in Jerusalem. They said to the authorities, 'Judge for yourselves whether it is right in God's sight to obey you rather than God' (Acts 4:19). But it is wrong to use God's Name to cover up something that is wrong, like those Jews who put aside their obligations to honour their parents by saying that money they might have given to them was 'Corban', that is, a gift devoted to God (Mark 7:11). Honouring our parents is a duty God plainly places upon us in the fifth commandment (Exodus 20:12). In a subtle way some first century Jews tried to wriggle out of this duty. Imagine a young man possessing money which he ought to have used to help his elderly parents. If he said of the money 'Corban' - 'it is a gift offered to God' - the Pharisees and teachers of the law laid it down that he could not change his mind. That money was no longer available for his parents' support. But the subtle deceit was that in practice the actual money or possessions did not then have to be offered to God. The vow easily became a legal fiction enabling individuals to retain the money for themselves. But what made matters worse was that they disgraced God's Name by introducing him into their conversation in such a despicable manner.

THE IMPORTANCE OF OUR WORSHIP

To hallow God's Name is to honour him by our worship. In worship as it ought to be we respond to God's disclosure of his Name in the Bible, and especially in its revelation in his Son. Worship then centres upon that revelation and is ordered by it. It is because God has exalted above all things his Name and his Word that we praise his Name for attributes like his love and faithfulness (Psalm 138:2) for the Scriptures reveal them. In worship we say to one another, 'Glorify the LORD with me: let us exalt his name together' (Psalm 34:3). Or, to quote the second verse of Timothy Dudley-Smith's paraphrase of the Magnificat:

Tell out my soul, the greatness of his Name!
Make known his might, the deeds his arm has done;
His mercy sure, from age to age the same;
His holy Name - the Lord, the Mighty One.

In worship our rightful absorption is with God himself and not with ourselves. The test of worship which hallows his Name is not whether or not it pleases us, but if it pleases him. The test of everything we do must be its conformity to God's will. God's people have always been in danger of losing sight of the proper preoccupation they should have with God himself in worship, rather than settling for what they themselves delight in or choose (Isaiah 1:29). Christians sadly move from church to church, and sometimes cause divisions over methods and expressions of worship. God's Name may be brought into disrepute by such behaviour. We have lost sight of the priority of God's honour if after a service we ask, 'Did you enjoy it?' More important questions are, 'Were God's people worshipping him in reality? And was God pleased with the worship offered?'

God's Name is not hallowed when worship becomes an excuse for focusing upon human personalities, or exercising spiritual gifts for our own enjoyment. The Corinthian church became so preoccupied with doing their own thing, and exercising personal gifts, that the God-ward aspect of worship became obscured. Paul longed instead that their corporate worship should so hallow God's Name that any outsider coming in would fall down and worship God, exclaiming 'God is really among you!' (1 Corinthians 14:25). Encouraging accounts have been given of the Church in China in spite of opposition and persecution. On one occasion as many as a thousand met together in a remote place, where they felt they would not be disturbed. Their meeting went on for several hours with teaching, singing and testimonies. A great sense of God's presence was evident. When the meeting ended five young men in the front stood up and said they had been sent to make arrests. They confessed that they had been so impressed by all they had heard and seen that they too wanted to believe.

The centrality of our Lord Jesus Christ, by whom God's Name has been perfectly made known to us, must never be assumed, since it is all too easy for our worship either to become routine, mechanical and slovenly or frothy, frivolous and irreverent. Do people come away from our services, declaring, 'Isn't God wonderful!' Or do they leave saying things like, 'Isn't he a talented musician or she a beautiful singer? Haven't we got a super band or orchestra?' If we put our enjoyment of worship before our honouring God, we remove God from his proper place, and cease being the kind of worshippers he seeks.

THE MOTIVATION OF EVANGELISM

The principal motivation for evangelism is the honouring or hallowing of God's Name: in evangelism we bring his Name before peoples and nations (Acts 9:15); we 'declare his glory among the nations, his marvellous deeds among all peoples' (Psalm 96:3). Paul made an interesting comment on the effect his own conversion had upon Christians in Judea when they heard of it: 'They only heard the report: "The man who formerly persecuted us is now preaching the faith he once tried to destroy." And they praised God because of me' (Galatians 1:23,24). They did not praise Paul, but they rightly praised God for what he had done in Paul. The verb for 'praise' is that from which we get our word doxology, and which is also used in Matthew 5:16 where our Lord speaks of our good works as God's children bringing praise to him.

We hallow and sanctify God's Name in evangelism by working to bring others to faith in our Lord Jesus, and then to discipleship. Evangelism is never an end in itself. Conversion is the prelude to worship of God and a life lived for him. We look beyond the benefit the individual gains personally through salvation to the glory he or she brings to God as a result of salvation. Paul significantly wrote of himself as 'a minister of Christ Jesus to the Gentiles with the priestly duty of proclaiming the gospel of God, so that the Gentiles might become an offering acceptable to God, sanctified by the Holy Spirit' (Romans 15:16).

Dr. Martyn Lloyd-Jones established what he called 'five foundation principles' of evangelism in a booklet entitled *The Presentation of the Gospel*, and point one was: 'The supreme object of this work is to glorify God ... The first object of preaching the gospel is not to save souls ... Nothing else, however good in itself, or however noble, must be allowed to usurp that first place.'

THE WITNESS OF OUR LIVES

To hallow God's Name is to bring credit to him by the way in which we live. This is the main thrust of this request interpreted by other Scriptures. In the Sermon on the Mount, of which this prayer is a part in Matthew's gospel, our Lord Jesus, having told his disciples that they were 'the light of the world', urged them, 'Let your light shine before men, that they may see your good deeds and praise your Father in heaven' (Matthew 5:16). God is praised - his Name is hallowed - as his children's deeds and behaviour are good. Our lives are to tell the world the truth about God, and when they do, his Name is hallowed. Bought with a price, God intends us to bring honour to him by our transformed character and conduct (1 Corinthians 6:20). Our relationship to him as his redeemed children has direct bearing upon our moral and ethical behaviour: immorality, for example, is ruled out in all its aspects - casual sex, adultery, child abuse, and homosexual practice.

We hallow God's Name by daily awareness of his holy nature. Joseph gave a good example of this when under severe pressure to commit adultery. Betrayed by jealous brothers and sold as a slave, he found himself far from home living as a servant in the house of an Egyptian. He proved himself so reliable and trustworthy that Potiphar, his master, put him in charge of his household, and entrusted to his care everything he owned. Joseph was well-built and handsome, and Potiphar's wife took notice of him, and said, 'Come to bed with me.' Joseph refused, and reminded his master's wife of the trust her husband placed in him. He then acknowledged God by declaring, 'How then could I do such a wicked thing and sin against God?' (Genesis 39:9). Joseph lost his job, but kept his integrity and testimony, and, most important of all, God's Name was hallowed. The Bible's plain teaching is that 'everyone who confesses the name of the Lord must turn away from wickedness' (2 Timothy 2:19).

One of the best means of hallowing God's Name is to undertake our daily employment with enthusiasm and diligence, setting the Lord Jesus Christ before us as the One we really want to please most of all in our work (Colossians 3:24). For this reason Paul urged the Colossians, many of whom were slaves, 'Whatever you do, whether in word or deed, do it all in the name of the Lord Jesus, giving thanks to the Father through him' (Colossians 3:17). We are to live such good lives that those who may oppose us on account of our Christian profession will be ashamed because they have nothing bad to say about us. We are to show that we can be fully trusted, so that in every way we do credit to the teaching about God our Saviour (Titus 2:8-10; cf. 1 Peter 2:12). Every working day has potential for hallowing God's Name. This lifts daily employment to a level where it becomes part of our worship of God.

It was reported in the first century that many a purchaser of slaves deliberately chose Christian slaves because of their reputation for giving good service. Imagine two masters discussing the best kind of slave to buy in the slave-market. One said to the other, 'What kind of slave are you hoping to purchase today?' 'Oh, the usual - one with youth on his side, good biceps, and healthy looking. What about you?' 'Oh,' answered the other, 'I want to ask questions about them first. Although I'm not a Christian myself, I'm looking for a Christian slave, because I've found Christian slaves hard-working, honest and reliable.' Such slaves, without knowing it, hallowed God's Name. People may not read the Bible but they read our lives. Our employers may not see us going to church but they watch how we work. A father may look at his son and say, 'He does me credit.' Our heavenly Father should be able to say that of our daily work.

Waldensian Christians, who took their name from Peter Waldo, a wealthy and devout merchant in Lyons in the 12th century, conspicuously honoured God by their good reputation, and their blamelessness passed into something of a proverb. Anyone who professed to love God, to honour Jesus Christ, and who at the same time was honest, and not a slanderer, swearer, liar, adulterer, murderer, thief or avenger, was immediately identified as a Waldensian. God's Name is hallowed in job interviews when employers are drawn to candidates - if they discover that they are Christians - because experience has proved that Christians turn out to be among the most reliable and conscientious employees. No wonder David declares in the twenty-third psalm, 'He guides me in paths of righteousness for his name's sake' (Psalm 23:3). Our behaviour either demonstrates or shames our Father's good name.

A CORPORATE ASPECT

To hallow God's Name is to bring credit to him by the way in which we live together as his people. Just as there is one God and Father of us all, so there is only one family of believers. Love for one another is the priority in our relationships together. The Lord Jesus spelt this out with searching clarity: 'A new command I give you: Love one another. As I have loved you, so you must love one another. All men will know that you are my disciples if you love one another' (John 13:34,35). Genuinely following the Lord Jesus, we discover a spirit of unity among ourselves, so that with one heart and mouth we glorify the God and Father of our Lord Jesus Christ (Romans 15:5,6).

Honour is not brought to God's Name by splits and divisions in his family over secondary matters, or supposedly doctrinal issues which are, if the truth be known, the consequence of the conflict of unsanctified personalities, not under the Lordship of Christ. The only person who rejoices in divisions is the evil one, for by them his kingdom is consolidated.

God's Name is praised when we put our differences right and accept one another as the Lord Jesus has accepted us (Romans 15:7). That may sometimes be extremely costly; but so what? Our desire is to hallow our Father's Name.

OUR LORD'S EXAMPLE

Our Lord Jesus is our example here as elsewhere: he always hallowed the Father's Name. He delighted in his Father's attributes. Words like 'Holy Father' (John 17:11), 'Righteous Father' (John 17:25), 'Abba, Father' (Mark 14:36) sprang naturally to his lips. Assured of access to his Father, and rejoicing in fellowship with him, he delighted in his Father's character, and lived his human life in the light of it. It is the Spirit of his Son God sends into our hearts, enabling us to call him 'Abba, Father' (Romans 8:15; Galatians 4:6).

'Father, glorify your name!' was the heart-beat of the Lord Jesus' prayers (John 12:28), no matter what the cost to himself. He hallowed the Father's Name by obedience to his Word, setting us an example to follow.

THE FEAR OF THE LORD

This first petition in the Lord's Prayer is consistent with the Bible's constant emphasis upon the fear of God. As Isaiah says, 'The LORD Almighty is the one you are to regard as holy, he is the one you are to fear' (Isaiah 8:13). The theme of the fear of the Lord appears frequently in the Psalms, and is often illustrated (Psalm 34:9; cf. 5:7; 15:4; 22:23). Rather afraid of the term, we tend to ignore it or water it down. Both approaches are wrong. Rather we need to explain what is meant by it and then teach it.

The fear of the Lord is not solely an Old Testament concept, although it finds its fullest exposition there. When the early Church knew spiritual blessing, Luke records, 'It was strengthened; and encouraged by the Holy Spirit, it grew in numbers, living in the fear of the Lord' (Acts 9:31). Old Testament books like Job, Psalms, Proverbs and Ecclesiastes set forth the fear of the Lord as the door through which God's wisdom comes to us (Job 28:28; Psalm 111:10; Proverbs 1:7; 9:10; Ecclesiastes 12:13). As we pray in the fear of the Lord, he gives us wisdom to ask from him what is right and appropriate.

An unconverted person's fear of God is often a fear of being punished; God's children, however, fear to offend him. The fear unbelievers have of God is usually prompted by unworthy thoughts of him. The fear believers have arises from a proper understanding and regard for his character, and an overwhelming desire as his children to please him, and not to grieve him. It is the reverence sons and daughters give to their heavenly Father in the view of his character. The fear of the Lord is not a troubling and terrifying fear but a reverential fear of him on account of his holiness. It is a worship of him which shows itself in a worshipping submission to him, and a genuine seeking after him. The fear of the Lord does not lead us to shun him, but to run to him (Psalm 34:9,10).

The fear of the Lord is the key to a treasure: as we practise it, we discover the super-abundance of God's salvation. It is a gloriously liberating principle, for fearing God we have nothing else to fear. As the delightful paraphrase of Psalm 34 puts it in the *Jubilate Hymns* version,

Fear him, you saints, and you will then
Have nothing else to fear;

His service shall be your delight,
Your needs shall be his care.

EFFECTIVE PRAYER

This petition provides a powerful motive and pointer to effective prayer. Do we face opposition to God's cause? Then remember that his Name is hallowed by the defeat of his enemies, when their faces are covered with shame as they discover that he alone is 'the Most High over all the earth' (Psalm 83:18; cf. 1 Kings 18:39).

When Moses reviewed God's dealings with Israel, and their disastrous rebellion against the Lord, he described the basis of his prayer to God for them: 'I lay prostrate before the LORD those forty days and nights because the LORD had said he would destroy you. I prayed to the LORD and said, "O Sovereign LORD, do not destroy your people, your own inheritance that you redeemed by your great power and brought out of Egypt with a mighty hand. Remember your servants Abraham, Isaac and Jacob. Overlook the stubbornness of this people, their wickedness and their sin. Otherwise, the country from which you brought us will say, 'Because the LORD was not able to take them into the land he had promised them, and because he hated them, he brought them out to put them to death in the desert.' But they are your people, your inheritance that you brought out by your great power and outstretched arm"' (Deuteronomy 9:25-29). Moses' concern was for the hallowing of God's Name. He recognised that what was at stake was not simply his people's survival but God's Name - his ability to keep his promises and to show his love for his people.

In prayer we call upon God's Name (Joel 2:32). True prayer is essentially our response to what we know about God himself, our almost automatic response to knowing and believing the truth about him. He has promised to be his people's shield, and calling upon his Name, therefore, may mean asking for his protection. He has revealed his love to us, and prayer - calling upon his Name - may appropriately be our casting ourselves upon his love. All God's attributes and promises encourage us to call upon him.

Are we struggling in our churches with problems which never ought to be difficulties? Let us cry, 'Help us, O God our Saviour, for the glory of your name; deliver us and forgive our sins for your name's sake' (Psalm 79:9).

Do we long that unconverted men and women should recognise God for who he is, and praise him? Let us then pray for ourselves with this end in view: 'May God be gracious to us and bless us and make his face shine upon us, that your ways be known on earth, your salvation among all nations.' (Psalm 67:1-2). 'Let them know that you, whose name is the LORD - that you alone are the Most High over all the earth' (Psalm 83:18).

OUR FIRST PURPOSE

'Hallowed be your Name' agrees with the first question and answer of the Shorter Catechism: 'What is man's chief end? It is to glorify God and to enjoy him forever.' Our principal desire should be that God should be glorified. We shall always feel in practice that we fall far short of this objective. Nevertheless we may pray as Robert Murray M'Cheyne, 'Lord, make me as holy as a saved sinner can be.' The ultimate end of our being, and every other, is the glorifying - or hallowing - of God's Name. 'For from him and through him and to him are all things. To him be the glory for ever! Amen' (Romans 11:36).

REVERENT WORSHIPPERS

Reverent worshippers is the second picture the Lord's Prayer provides of what it means to be a Christian. As reverent worshippers, at the heart of our prayers is the cry, 'Hallowed be your Name.' The Father seeks those who worship him in spirit and in truth, who, mindful of his holiness, honour and worship him with awe and reverential fear (John 4:23,24; Hebrews 12:28,29).

Chapter 3

Loyal citizens

'Your kingdom come'

The Lord is King! The Bible constantly declares God's Kingship (Psalm 5:2; 84:3; 89:18; 98:6). He 'is King for ever and ever' (Psalm 10:16), the great King over all the earth (Psalm 47:2,7; cf. Psalm 95:3). He 'has established his throne in heaven, and his kingdom rules over all' (Psalm 103:19). Although men and women in their folly may feel that they can rebel against his kingship, it is a vain endeavour. As the second psalm begins, 'Why do the nations conspire and the people plot in vain?'

Early on in the book bearing his name, the prophet Isaiah enters the Temple. The timing was significant because it was in the year that King Uzziah died (6:1). Humanly speaking, the nation of Judah was at a low ebb, and much seemed out of control. So far as the nation's throne was concerned, its occupant had been removed by death. But Isaiah's entry into the Temple was memorable and significant because he was given a vision of another throne - one superior to every other and with authority over all others. On that throne Isaiah saw the Lord seated, 'the King, the LORD Almighty' (Isaiah 6:1,5). God's Kingship influenced all Isaiah subsequently wrote. It particularly binds together the first thirty-seven chapters. Isaiah's vision in the Temple of the Lord, 'the King, the LORD Almighty' (Isaiah 6:5), is matched by the New Testament assertion that he is 'the blessed and only Ruler, the King of kings, and Lord of lords, who alone is immortal and who lives in unapproachable light, whom no-one has seen or can see' (1 Timothy 6:15,16).

GOD RULES

God's kingdom is not to be thought of in the way we think of human kingdoms, whose boundaries change, whose kings and queens are deposed or die, and whose power grows or declines. In Old Testament times kingdoms like those of the Babylonians and Assyrians seemed indestructible; now they are but a memory! At the time the New Testament came into being Rome gave every appearance of invincibility, but now Latin is a 'dead' language and Roman civilisation at best talked about when ancient history is studied. Likewise, Hitler's Third Reich appeared unstoppable at the time. But it ended in defeat and disgrace. God's kingdom is above all others: it endures when the rest wane: 'Your kingdom is an everlasting kingdom, and your dominion endures through all generations' (Psalm 145:13; cf. Daniel 4:3,34). God's kingdom is synonymous with his kingship. It is a way of saying that 'Heaven rules' - that is to say, 'God rules' (Daniel 4:26)!

Since God already exercises a universal dominion, in praying, 'Your kingdom come,' we are asking for something different and specific, which is not yet complete. What we have in view is the kingdom of his Son, the Messiah.

OLD TESTAMENT ANTICIPATION

The Old Testament anticipated the Messiah's kingdom. In Psalm 2 the Messiah is shown to be the King God has appointed (6), with a universal kingdom (8). Isaiah's prophecies concerning the Messiah have his kingdom clearly in view: chapters 1-37 focus upon the Messiah as King and chapters 56-66 as the Anointed Conqueror. 'Of the increase of his government and peace there will be no end. He will reign on David's throne and over his kingdom, establishing and upholding it with justice and righteousness' (Isaiah 9:7). All that he does will be marked by wisdom, understanding, counsel and power (Isaiah 11:2). The effects of his reign will be dramatic, not least in regard to nature and creation: 'The wolf will live with the lamb, the leopard will lie down with the goat, the calf and the lion and the yearling together; and a little child will lead them. The cow will feed with the bear, their young will lie down together, and the lion will eat straw like the ox. The infant will play near the hole of the cobra, and the young child will put his hand into the viper's nest' (Isaiah 11:6-8; cf. Hosea 2:18; Romans

8:18ff). Eden will be restored. The Messiah's dominion will be world-wide (Isaiah 11:10-16).

Daniel spoke of the Messiah's kingdom as a rock 'cut out, but not by human hands' (Daniel 2:34). Micah adds his contribution to the picture of the coming Messiah-King: 'But you, Bethlehem Ephrathah, though you are small among the clans of Judah, out of you will come for me one who will be ruler over Israel, whose origins are from of old, from ancient times. ... He will stand and shepherd his flock in the strength of the LORD, in the majesty of the name of the LORD his God. And they will live securely, for then his greatness will reach to the ends of the earth' (Micah 5:2,4).

Zechariah urges, 'Rejoice greatly, O Daughter of Zion! Shout, Daughter of Jerusalem! See, your king comes to you, righteous and having salvation, gentle and riding on a donkey, on a colt, the foal of a donkey' (Zechariah 9:9). Malachi speaks of the Messiah King as being 'like a refiner's fire or a launderer's soap', or as 'a refiner and purifier of silver' who will expose all that is wrong (Malachi 3:2,3).

THE KINGDOM OF HEAVEN AND THE KINGDOM OF GOD

The kingdom of God was a central theme of Jesus' teaching in the first three gospels. The phrase itself occurs 14 times in Mark, 32 in Luke and 4 in Matthew. Matthew substitutes the 'kingdom of heaven' in its place. The two terms are, in effect, the same. 'Heaven' was a common Jewish substitute for God's Name in that as a sign of respect for his Name they used an alternative. We find this way of referring to God's Name in the story of the prodigal son who, in declaring his repentance, said to his father, 'I have sinned against heaven and against you' (Luke 15:18) - 'heaven' standing for God. Matthew probably preferred 'kingdom of heaven' out of sensitivity to his Jewish readers.

GOD'S KINGDOM AND THE KINGDOM OF HIS SON

We need draw no distinction between God's kingdom - the kingdom of heaven - and the kingdom of his Son. Daniel prophesied, 'The God of heaven will set up a kingdom that will never be destroyed' (Daniel 2:44), and Daniel saw that this kingdom was to be subjected to the Messiah: 'In my vision at night I looked, and there before me was one like a son of man, coming with the clouds of heaven. He approached the Ancient of Days and was led into his presence. He was given authority, glory and sovereign power; all peoples, nations and men of every language worshipped him. His dominion is an everlasting dominion that will not pass away, and his kingdom is one that will never be destroyed' (Daniel 7:13,14).

Behind this prophecy is what we sometimes call 'the covenant of redemption'. It is a pity that the term is not used and elaborated upon as it was by the Puritans and older theologians. It tries to put into words the wonder and mystery of God's plan of salvation, a purpose which preceded the fall and even the world's creation.

Clearly human rebellion did not take God by surprise, since he is omniscient and knows the end from the beginning. (As I write about this I feel the limitations of human understanding and language.) The decision was made in the eternal counsels of the Father, the Son and the Holy Spirit not to destroy the whole of humankind because of sin. Rather it was determined that salvation would be provided.

This purpose of salvation involved a division of office and allocation of function within the three Persons of the Trinity. The Father was the first mover: the purpose and plan was his. The Son willingly subordinated himself to the Father to carry it out, and the Spirit likewise to applying it to needy sinners.

The Lord Jesus undertook to suffer what was due to his people, the elect, and to do what was required to be done on their behalf, that they might be delivered, reconciled and accepted with God. He has therefore received on his people's behalf all God's promises of grace, and eternal benefits and privileges. Part of the covenant of redemption is that as a fruit of his saving work for his people, God the Father conferred the title of King on his Son. Psalm 2 - a Messianic psalm - uniquely expresses this truth. God the Father is heard to say, 'I have installed my King on Zion, my holy hill' (Psalm 2:6), and he says to his Son, 'Ask of me, and I will make the nations your inheritance, the ends of the earth your possession. You will rule them with an iron sceptre; you will dash them to pieces like pottery' (Psalm 2:8,9).

As Christians we acknowledge the Lord Jesus to be our King, and we demonstrate that Kingship in our lives. First, he brought us into glad submission to his kingship by his Spirit as we were brought to repentance and faith in him. Now he rules and defends us, restrains and conquers all our enemies. As our King we delight to honour, confess, obey and worship him.

Having died for our sins, and risen victoriously over death, our Lord Jesus ascended to heaven as King. Throughout the centuries Christians have rejoiced to take up words of Psalm 24 as appropriate to this glorious moment: 'Lift up your heads, O you gates; be lifted up, you ancient doors, that the King of glory may come in. Who is this King of glory? The LORD strong and mighty, the LORD mighty in battle. Lift up your heads, O you gates; lift them up, you ancient doors, that the King of glory may come in. Who is he, this King of glory? The LORD Almighty - he is the King of glory' (Psalm 24:7-10). At our Saviour's return we shall gaze in wonder and admiration at the glory and power of his Kingdom, and the authority the Father has given him (Revelation 11:15; 12:10). The climax of the whole plan of redemption will be when our Lord Jesus 'hands over the kingdom to God the Father after he has destroyed all dominion, authority and power' (1 Corinthians 15:24).

The covenant of redemption reminds us that the initiative in the whole plan of salvation was the Father's, and that there is a particular order of relationship between the Persons of the Trinity. The Father is first; the Son is second: he is begotten of the Father and is sent by him. The Spirit is third: he proceeds from the Father and the Son. God the Father gave us his Son to be the Mediator and Saviour. It was the Father who exalted him on the completion of his saving work to his right hand and committed to him the government of the world in the interests of the Church. But the goal of it all is the acknowledgment of the Son to the glory of the Father (Philippians 2:11), when God will 'be all in all' (1 Corinthians 15:28). This is not to say that our Lord Jesus shall cease to reign or have a kingdom for the Scriptures declare that 'his kingdom will never end' (Luke 1:33) and 'will never be destroyed' (Daniel 7:14).

Our Lord Jesus has therefore a threefold kingdom. First, he is King because he is God, the Second Person of the Trinity, a rule and kingship he can never abdicate. Second, because of his Incarnation and finished work on behalf of his Church, he is King over his people. Thirdly, at his Resurrection and Ascension, he was exalted to a position of dominion, in which all power in heaven and earth is committed to his hands until the work of redemption reaches its climax and the total subjection of his enemies is complete. We do not yet see all his enemies put under his feet. The task the Father has given him is to defeat sin, to overcome death and to liberate men and women. When that work of abolishing all forces opposed to God is complete, he will deliver up the dominion he has over the world as the Father's delegate or representative, that the great design of the whole plan of salvation shall be accomplished - the glory of the Father. We cannot grasp all that means, but that is how it is declared. When it happens, we shall understand!

TWO DIFFERENT BUT COMPLEMENTARY TRUTHS

Two different yet complementary truths emerge in the New Testament's teaching about the kingdom. God's kingdom refers first to his kingship - his absolute sovereignty. God's sovereignty is not so much an attribute of God, but a consequence of all his attributes.

Although the world in general rebels against God, he has not relinquished his sovereignty, but is in control as he works out his unchanging purposes in human affairs. It is true that there are times when in our ignorance God seems to be no more about the world. Nevertheless, 'Our God is in heaven; he does whatever pleases him' (Psalm 115:3). Whatever happens in the world, God is on his heavenly throne, in complete control (Psalm 11:4). His sovereignty is absolute.

He is sovereign in history over the affairs of the nations: he but 'whistles for those at the ends of the earth' and they come 'swiftly and speedily' (Isaiah 5:26). He, the Holy One, can use even evil men or nations to carry out his purposes (Isaiah 10:5-19). He can so utilise the decisions and actions of a heathen ruler like Cyrus that he can declare,

'He is my shepherd' (Isaiah 44:28). He may be behind the actions of men, when they do not realise it (Jonah 2:3). All his creatures combine to do his will as he determines (Jonah 4:6-8). His is the sovereignty of both a potter and a father (Isaiah 45:9-13). The nations are but instruments in his hands to do as he pleases (Isaiah 10:5); yet at the same time his instruments are morally responsible (Isaiah 10:5-15). His sovereignty guarantees that history will end up as he purposes: it gives complete security to all his promises. His sovereignty means that he is at work in the ordinary everyday affairs of life, and of the nations, in accordance with his unchanging principles of righteousness and justice.

The doctrine of God's sovereignty is not popular. It undermines human pride which loves to feel that it is in control. Jonathan Edwards (1703-1758), a great philosopher and theologian, found that from childhood his mind had been full of objections against the teaching of God's sovereignty. But he wrote, 'There has been a wonderful alteration in my mind ... The doctrine has very often appeared exceedingly pleasant, bright, and sweet. Absolute sovereignty is what I love to ascribe to God. But my first conviction was not so.' God's sovereignty is the foundation of the three great truths of justification, sanctification and glorification (Romans 8:28-30). It provides confidence for evangelism and glorious assurance for the future.

Whatever happens, God is on his heavenly throne, in complete control (Psalm 9:11; 47:7). He rules and overcomes all his enemies. The First Cause holds all second causes in his hand: 'The LORD foils the plans of the nations; he thwarts the purposes of the peoples. But the plans of the LORD stand firm for ever, the purposes of his heart throughout all generations' (Psalm 33:10,11). This truth is as relevant to the individual as it is to nations. The Book of Ruth, for instance, is significant for the way in which it shows that God works out his purposes in the small details of the lives of seemingly unimportant people (e.g. Ruth 2:3).

Confidence in God's sovereignty cures pessimism. With our lives in his sure care, we may be confident that we will lack nothing good (Psalm 34:9,10; cf. 84:11; Deuteronomy 6:24; 8:3; Romans 8:28,37). When we do not understand God's delays, the right attitude is 'I will wait patiently' (Habbakuk 3:16). If you were lost in an area where you had never been before, and where you did not even know the language, it would be an incredible relief to meet a friend who knew the way perfectly, and could take you to your destination by the safest and quickest route. With the Sovereign Lord as our guide, both our journey and destination are secure.

But God's kingdom refers secondly to what God is doing among the nations through the saving work of his Son, his King. The kingdom in this use of the term is more or less the same as salvation. Through the merits of his Son's atoning blood, God rescues men and women 'from the dominion of darkness' and brings them 'into the kingdom of the Son he loves' (Colossians 1:13). He makes them fit 'to share in the inheritance of the saints in the kingdom of light' (Colossians 1:12). This is New Testament 'kingdom' theology.

As Jesus went through the towns and villages of Israel he preached 'the good news of the kingdom' (Matthew 9:35; Luke 8:1). He said, 'The time has come. The kingdom of heaven is near. Repent, and believe the good news!' (Mark 1:15; cf. Matthew 4:17). It is this kingdom we have particularly in mind when we pray, 'Your Kingdom come!'

ESSENTIALLY A SPIRITUAL KINGDOM

The danger in recent decades - and perhaps for longer - has been to neglect the spiritual nature of God's kingdom, and to put something else in its place. Jesus' emphasis - and that of the whole of the Bible - is upon the spiritual and inward character of God's kingdom and rule in human lives.

A reason for caution over the years in using the term 'the kingdom of God' has been its misuse or misapplication. Theological liberalism of the late nineteenth and early twentieth centuries majored on what became known as 'the social gospel', regarding the kingdom of God as identical with the achievement of social change.

The advocates of the social gospel protested against any form of Christianity that saw God as interested in less than the total human situation. It tended to coincide with limited views of the Bible's inspiration and authority, and defective grasp of the truth of Jesus' deity and of the fundamental nature of his substitutionary death. Jesus was seen as simply a perfect man and great teacher. His Sermon on the Mount was thought of as something that could be put into Acts of Parliament and turned into laws, with a view to establishing God's kingdom on earth. The kingdom was then seen as wider than the Church, and our responsibility as that of working with God for the transformation of the social order. Speaking generally, it underestimated human sinfulness and overlooked fundamentals of the gospel.

The social gospel was optimistic about perfecting the human condition, and sometimes there was an underlying confidence in the evolution for good of human nature so that things must get better and better. But there was a great mixture of opinions: while some regarded conversion as superfluous, others viewed it as a short-cut to social reform. The social gospel was seen by some as an evangelistic strategy to reach the working classes, and a dimension of Christian mission. The argument in essence was: if we do not show ourselves concerned about bad housing and better homes, those who live in bad housing and poor homes will not be attracted by our message.

Identified with God's will for the social order, the kingdom of God was viewed as an obtainable ideal, here and now. Similar ideas continually raise their head since there is nothing new under the sun. As with most false emphases there is a measure of truth within them of which we need to take notice if we are to maintain our integrity. We cannot separate true religion - the religion which the gospel promotes - from feeding the hungry, rescuing and welcoming the refugee and standing up for those whom society wrongly treats on account of race and colour. 'Religion that God our Father accepts as pure and faultless is this: to look after orphans and widows in their distress and to keep oneself from being polluted by the world' (James 1:27). Words alone are not enough; action is required (James 2:15-18).

Christians always have to wrestle with problems of priorities, and we can never say that we have got it exactly right. Spirituality and social concern are not opposites, although sometimes that may have appeared to be the case. Social concern is a proper outcome of the gospel, and is not to be divorced from it. New men and women in Christ should show a new social concern that will mean that they feed the hungry and thirsty, show kindness to strangers, clothe the needy, and visit the sick and those in prison (Matthew 25:35-36). We are never to forget the physical needs of our fellow human beings.

Following hard upon the heels of the social gospel, in third world countries, notably in parts of South America, liberation theology developed, which thinks of God's kingdom in political terms, and argues for radical social change in the name of the gospel. It reinterprets the whole of theology from the standpoint of liberation. Salvation and the kingdom of God are then seen to have everything to do with this world, but little or nothing with the next. The kingdom of God is seen as a process of evolution, with history creating a new humanity.

Living as we do - and as all our predecessors have done - in an unjust, savage and hungry world, we cannot be indifferent to people's economic, social and political needs. But important qualifications must be made. First, we do not anticipate God's kingdom being set up here on earth in terms of economic, social and political equality. Until our Saviour's coming, injustice, inequality and all that goes with them will continue: Satan, the god of this world, sees to that. This sad truth provides neither room for complacency nor excuse for not doing our best to relieve acute human needs found throughout the world. But we do not imagine that the transformation we long for is going to take place apart from the coming of the King.

Secondly, our Lord Jesus carefully resisted pressures to think in this way of his Messianic kingdom. The most vivid illustration is the feeding of the five thousand, the only miracle recorded in all four gospels, and given in greatest detail in John 6. It is difficult to know how much significance there may be in the information that the men sat down in groups of hundreds and fifties (Mark 6:39,40), for it almost seems as if they sat down in ranks, ready for instant military mobilization. Jesus knew 'that they intended to come and make him king by force'; so he 'withdrew again to a mountain by himself' (John 6:15). He then did two noteworthy things: first, he sent both the disciples and the crowds away; secondly, when he next met up with the crowds, he deliberately spoke not about bread for the body, but bread that saves the soul - his broken body. He could not have stressed more the spiritual nature of his Messiahship and the centrality to it of his substitutionary death. 'Jesus said to them, "I tell you the truth, unless you eat the flesh of the Son of Man and drink his blood, you have no life in you. Whoever eats my flesh and drinks my blood has eternal life, and I will raise him up at the last day. For my flesh is real food and my blood is real drink. Whoever eats my flesh and drinks my blood remains in me, and I in him. Just as the living Father sent me and I live because of the Father, so the one who feeds on me will live because of me. This is the bread that came down from heaven. Your forefathers ate manna and died, but he who feeds on this bread will live for ever"' (John 6:53-58).

This emphasis conformed exactly with his manifesto which he declared at his ministry's commencement in the synagogue in Nazareth. He read the prophet Isaiah: 'The Spirit of the Lord is on me, because he has anointed me to preach good news to the poor. He has sent me to proclaim freedom for the prisoners and recovery of sight for the blind, to release the oppressed, to proclaim the year of the Lord's favour' (Luke 4:18-19). Jesus was never indifferent to those who were literally poor, prisoners, blind and oppressed, but his ministry and teaching always stressed the spiritual nature of his mission.

Thirdly, the way in which the kingdom of God influences society for good is by the impact of its individual members' lives, as they reflect and display God's holiness and love. The power of this cannot be calculated, and we cannot imagine what the world would be like without it. The battle in Parliament fought by Wilberforce and others in the nineteenth century to bring about the abolition of slavery in the British colonies, is an example. For Christians to take such action in the first century was impossible. The only machinery then would have been rebellion, leading to mass bloodshed, and that is not the Christian way. Such a recourse had failed when tried by others. An alternative some Christians opted for was actually to purchase the individual freedom of slaves. But the most important contribution was to change for the better the relationship between masters and slaves. (The little letter of Paul to Philemon about the latter's runaway slave is a good example.)

When an owner of slaves was taught to regard his newly-converted slave as 'a dear brother' (Philemon 16), to 'provide' his slaves 'with what is right and fair' (Colossians 4:1) and to give a wage that was pleasing to God (James 5:1-6), then things could only get better - and they did!

The same is true with regard to the place of women in society. The Church today is sometimes pilloried for its attitude to women, but there is another side to the picture. Christians who followed Jesus' teaching, as, for example, in the Sermon on the Mount, found their attitudes in sex-ethics changed dramatically for the good. Furthermore, the gospel was addressed as clearly to women as to men: something expected by us, but not in the first century, for then they were very much the second sex, less than second class citizens. The gospel taught - and teaches - that men and women are of identical value in God's sight and may equally enter into his salvation in Jesus Christ (Galatians 3:28). Women like Phoebe, Lydia, Priscilla and others had a leading part in the gospel's spread. The Lord Jesus and his apostles championed women's rights when they taught that faithfulness and chastity are required as much of men as of women.

If the Sermon on the Mount may be viewed as the manifesto of the kingdom, then its members influence society most by their lives. The Sermon begins with the Beatitudes which set forth the proper character of those who belong to the kingdom (Matthew 5:1-12). The Sermon proceeds thereafter to talk of the kingdom - that is, of its members - functioning as salt and light by means of their conduct and good works (Matthew 5:13-16). The rest of the Sermon unfolds the practical implications.

Since the concept of the kingdom of God is so important for our understanding of God's purposes, we must not let its misuse rob us of its proper use.

A KINGSHIP IN OUR HEARTS

With us the heart represents especially the emotions. But in the Greek use of the term in the New Testament it stands for the centre or core of our whole being and personality: it is 'the wellspring of life' (Proverbs 4:23). It sums up our emotions, intellect and will. It is in our heart that our direction in life is set and our basic commitments decided (Jeremiah 17:9; Luke 6:45). To 'set apart Christ as Lord' in our 'hearts' (1 Peter 3:15) represents a complete revolution in our lives. Our feelings, longings, ambitions, decisions, thoughts, love, commitment and character come under his glad control. It is a kingdom totally unlike any other.

None can better define the kingdom than the King! The Lord Jesus taught that we enter God's kingdom only by new birth, and as a consequence of that miracle he actively rules as King in our hearts. He made plain to Nicodemus, a member of the Jewish ruling council, that to enter the kingdom of God he needed to be born again (John 3:3-7), 'born not of natural descent, nor of human decision or a husband's will, but born of God' (John 1:13). What is made of flesh and blood alone cannot share in God's kingdom (1 Corinthians 15:50); instead, God's all-powerful Spirit must work a miracle in our hearts. Our pride must be humbled, and we must receive the kingdom like little children, who have nothing to bring except our total dependence upon God's grace in Jesus Christ (Mark 10:14,15; Luke 18:16,17).

Many of Jesus' parables were about the kingdom, and they underline its importance. The parable of the sower describes how we enter it, and how God's rule in our life begins: we respond with obedience to Jesus' message (Mark 4:1-12). The parable of the weeds (Matthew 13:24-30, 36-43) shows that the kingdom of God does not grow without opposition from Satan. The parables of the mustard seed and the yeast illustrate the growth and penetration of the kingdom (Matthew 13:31-35): its beginnings may be small but its growth is irresistible.

The parables of the treasure and the pearl point to the incalculable worth of the kingdom (Matthew 13:44-46), since finding it is finding Jesus. None can measure the value of this discovery (Philippians 3:7-9). The parable of the ten virgins looks forward to the great day of the kingdom when Jesus returns (Matthew 25:1-13); and the parables of the talents and the coins indicate the kingdom's rewards (Matthew

25:14-30; Luke 19:12-27). The latter have nothing to do with earning salvation, since it is a free gift. But when we have received God's gift of salvation, the Lord Jesus chooses to reward faithful service. Those born into God's kingdom understand these parables; but those who remain outside of it tend to find them either a mystery or to misunderstand them altogether.

Jesus' Kingship in our hearts brings the blessings of salvation. As we acknowledge him as King we know his daily forgiveness (1 John 1:9). As we submit to his Kingship, we discover his will for our lives. As we seek first his kingdom, we are freed from fretful anxiety about material possessions, and, learning to be content, we delight in the glorious things he does for us (Matthew 6:33; Luke 12:31).

MAY YOUR KINGDOM COME IN PEOPLE'S LIVES

When we pray, 'Your Kingdom come!' we are praying first, therefore, that God's kingdom may come in people's lives, that men and women may be brought to repentance, so that they turn from rebellion against God, and believe on the King who died to be the Saviour.

God's kingdom came to a tax-collector called Zacchaeus as he met the King and, believing in him, turned from his sin and sought salvation (Luke 19:9). It came to a business woman, a dealer in purple cloth by the name of Lydia, as she listened to the apostle Paul on the banks of the river at Philippi, and the Lord opened her heart to pay attention to the good news of Jesus (Acts 16:14). We pray in the Lord's Prayer for that to happen in the lives of individuals, and especially those whom we know and for whom we have spiritual accountability.

God's kingdom came in the lives of thousands of people on the Day of Pentecost in Jerusalem, as the King, once crucified but now risen and ascended, was proclaimed. People 'were cut to the heart and said to Peter and the other apostles, "Brothers, what shall we do?"' Told by Peter to repent, believe and acknowledge God's King, his Messiah, 'those who accepted his message were baptised, and about three thousand were added to their number that day' (Acts 2:41). We pray for that to happen today! Our sovereign

Father can save not just in ones and twos but in thousands!

In praying, 'Your kingdom come' we pray, therefore, for conversions, and all that will accelerate God's kingdom - including the outpouring of the Holy Spirit in revival. Revival is an extraordinary work of God's Spirit when God comes down in power to his Church. Two consequences are conspicuous: Christian believers in general are spiritually invigorated and numerous unbelievers are brought to living faith in the Lord Jesus and are converted. The external circumstances of revival do not have to be identical with those that have previously taken place, but in all revivals God extends his kingdom and glorifies his Name. In times of revival God's kingdom is apparent. His command to repent is obeyed. His call to believe the good news of the gospel is both heard and heeded. The shout of the King is among his people. As we look at our neighbours and think of all unconverted peoples of the world, we should pray, 'Your kingdom come!'

The petitions, 'Hallowed be your Name,' and 'Your will be done' go together. Never is God's Name more honoured than when men and women praise and testify to his grace in saving them from Satan's kingdom and bringing them into that of his dear Son, Jesus Christ.

When God's kingdom comes in our lives - when his King, Jesus Christ our Lord, reigns in our hearts - a revolution happens. 'We take captive every thought to make it obedient to Christ' (2 Corinthians 10:5), and in our hearts we acknowledge him as Lord (1 Peter 3:15). The Beatitudes, with which the Sermon on the Mount begins, describe the intended character of the kingdom's citizens. Our lives are changed for the better: immorality, impurity, greed, hatred, discord, jealousy, bad temper, selfishness, dissensions, party spirit and envy, drunkenness, orgies and the like are **out**, and love, joy, peace, patience, kindness, goodness, faithfulness, gentleness and self-control are **in**!

The word 'fruit' by which these virtues are described (Galatians 5:22) reminds us that they do not appear overnight: they require time to grow. Pictures of the kingdom which our Saviour gave imply the same lesson - like the mustard seed and the leaven. At first like a grain of mustard seed we may have some small awareness of sin, and a correspondingly small consciousness of the power of our Saviour's blood, but as the seed grows these both increase. To begin with we may have little insight into the amazing depths of God's love, a love to which we respond with love and obedience. But as that insight grows, so does our joy, peace and zeal. They are all like mustard seeds which possess the capacity for growth to great trees. The leaven of the kingdom spreads continually to every part of our life, although sometimes imperceptibly.

What the present coming of God's kingdom means is illustrated in the requests that follow in the Lord's Prayer. God's kingdom comes as his will is done in our lives. His kingdom comes as we live in dependence upon him. His kingdom comes as we know his daily forgiveness and exercise it towards others. His kingdom comes as we want him to direct our lives and to deliver us from evil. In praying for his kingdom to come, we are asking that these benefits may be clearly seen, 'for the kingdom of God is not a matter of talk but of power' (1 Corinthians 4:20; Romans 14:17). Birth into God's kingdom brings us into the service of a new Master, and, in praying this prayer, we are asking that there may be no turning back, for 'no-one who puts his hand to the plough and looks back is fit for service in the kingdom of God' (Luke 9:62).

A FUTURE KINGDOM

The kingdom is both present and approaching. Our Lord Jesus spoke of the kingdom of God, secondly, as an inheritance believers possess in the future. It is identical with the age to come (Matthew 8:11; Mark 9:47; 10:23-25; 14:25; Luke 13:28). 'I confer on you a kingdom,' the Lord Jesus said to his disciples, 'just as my Father conferred one on me, so that you may eat and drink at my table in my kingdom and sit on thrones, judging the twelve tribes of Israel' (Luke 22:29,30). This promise was not made to them alone but to all believers. The Lord Jesus will say to the whole of his people, 'Come, you who are blessed by my Father; take your inheritance, the kingdom prepared for you since the creation of the world' (Matthew 25:34).

To the world at large we may, as God's children, not seem of much note, but it is the Father's pleasure to give us a place in his eternal kingdom. God has 'chosen those who are poor in the eyes of the world to be rich in faith and to inherit the kingdom he promised to those who love him' (James 2:5). In calling us into the fellowship of his Son, God calls us 'into his kingdom and glory' (1 Thessalonians 2:12). 'We are receiving a kingdom that cannot be shaken' (Hebrews 12:28). The writer of Hebrews takes up Haggai's prophecy that God will 'shake the heavens and the earth and the sea and the dry land' (Haggai 2:6). Inspired by the Holy Spirit, the writer interprets this to mean that God is going to shake his whole creation. When he does so, all this present creation will disappear, and only that which is permanent will remain - the kingdom of God to which all who are Jesus Christ's belong (Hebrews 12:26-28).

We see here, therefore, God's great and ultimate purpose: the revelation of his unshakeable kingdom. Let us picture a house being built. At first, we are most aware of the scaffolding, and it may be fairly impressive. But the purpose of the scaffolding is to bring about the erection of a building - the scaffolding is not an end in itself. When the building is complete, the scaffolding is, as it were, 'shaken': it is taken to bits and removed, but the building remains. What we witness in the work of the Church is but the scaffolding of God's great building operation. This world is the present sphere in which God is calling men and women to himself through Jesus Christ to belong to his eternal kingdom. Soon he will shake the earth and the heavens: the earth, this world - the scaffolding - will disappear. But the kingdom - God's building - will remain. How wonderful it is to know that we belong to God's kingdom that cannot be shaken (Hebrews 12:28)! The New Testament exercises great restraint in describing the kingdom since it is too wonderful to be put into words. We can echo in a spiritual sense the words of Psalm 137, which Jews used of their desire to be in Jerusalem: 'May my tongue cling to the roof of my mouth if I do not remember you, if I do not consider Jerusalem my highest joy' (verse 6).

We have no need to fear death for God will bring us safely to the eternal kingdom of our Lord and Saviour and his rich welcome (2 Timothy 4:18; 2 Peter 1:11). Daniel anticipated this: 'The saints of the Most High will receive the kingdom and will possess it for ever - yes, for ever and ever' (Daniel 7:18). The very thought of that heavenly kingdom produced in Paul a doxology: 'To him be glory for ever and ever. Amen' (2 Timothy 4:18). The kingdom will not have finally come until all its members have been gathered in, and its every enemy placed under our Saviour's feet (1 Corinthians 15:25), and all its citizens perfected in glory (Philippians 3:21).

Our membership of this kingdom is so assured that Christian believers are described as having their citizenship there already. When Paul wrote, 'Our citizenship is in heaven' (Philippians 3:20) it registered with his readers, the Philippians, probably more than it immediately does with us, although the truth is just as relevant. Philippi was a Roman colony. It was like a little piece of Rome transplanted from Rome itself. The streets, the practices, the customs and the standards of behaviour were entirely Roman. To live as a Roman citizen in Philippi was like living in Rome itself. So it ought to be for us with regard to our heavenly citizenship. Our heavenly citizenship should make us better citizens here and now in this world, whether in our diligence in paying taxes and law-keeping in general or in our desire to show love for our neighbour.

JUSTICE WILL BE DONE, AND RIGHTEOUSNESS WILL REIGN

The kingly reign that is God's, and has always been his, will be revealed at the final disclosure of his kingdom. The judgment of the wicked will take place, and every hostile power will be seen to be subject to him. The wonder of believers' salvation will be exhibited and the glorious redemption of the whole of creation from evil.

This prayer - 'Your kingdom come' - has pointed relevance to the wicked and violent world in which we live. On Sunday, 25th July 1993 1000 people were gathered at St. James's Church, Cape Town, for the evening service. A hooded man burst in, carrying a semi-automatic rifle and started firing indiscriminately at the congregation. Then two accomplices threw hand grenades into the crowded audience. Eleven were killed and many seriously injured. In a statement issued by one of the church leaders immediately afterwards he declared, 'While as Christians we must live in this fallen world, we do so knowing that at the end there is a new world coming when Jesus will be acknowledged to be King. The members of St. James's seek no revenge and harbour no bitterness. We are content to leave justice in the hands of the Almighty who has appointed a day of judgment when all will have to give account of their actions to him.'

We would be dishonest if we did not declare that we long for that day, when not only will justice be done, but perfect peace will exist and all the consequences of man's fall in Eden will be reversed. In this petition we pray for it!

THE COMING OF THE KING!

The full disclosure of the splendour of our Saviour's kingdom awaits his coming. When he appears from heaven, he will not return as the Suffering Saviour but as the glorious King. For many there will then be weeping and gnashing of teeth when they see Abraham, Isaac, and Jacob and all the prophets in the kingdom of God, and they themselves thrown out. Then Christian believers from east and west, and north and south, will take their places at the feast in the kingdom of heaven (Matthew 8:11; Luke 13:29).

The visible establishment of God's reign over all hostile powers will be seen. We will be able to say to God then, 'The time has come for judging the dead, and for rewarding your servants the prophets and your saints and those who reverence your name, both small and great - and for destroying those who destroy the earth' (Revelation 11:18).

When we are spiritually healthy, we eagerly anticipate our Saviour's return. The early Christians' watchword was 'Come, O Lord!' - 'Maranatha' (1 Corinthians 16:22). The New Testament draws to a close with the Risen Lord Jesus saying, 'Yes, I am coming soon' and his people, the Church, the Body and Bride of Christ, saying, 'Amen. Come, Lord Jesus' (Revelation 22:20). To know the Lord Jesus is to love him. To love him is to want to see him. To love him is to want to be with him. To love him, therefore, is to love his appearing. 'We eagerly await a Saviour' from heaven (Philippians 3:20).

There are aspects of his coming which I do not understand, but of its certainty I am in no doubt. What I cannot explain I do well to leave alone; but what I am sure about I must affirm. There are aspects of his coming - the most important - of which I am absolutely certain. It will be personal, physical, visible, sudden, glorious, and will usher his people into his everlasting kingdom. Perhaps significantly, those who mistakenly stress the present fulfilment of the kingdom in changed social order tend to be those who do not believe in the literal Second Coming of our Lord Jesus Christ.

A PRAYER WHICH DEMANDS OUR ACTIVE OBEDIENCE

The present coming of God's kingdom in people's lives is his prerogative, but he chooses to bring it about by his people's obedience. For the crowds on the Day of Pentecost in Jerusalem to enter the kingdom, the King had to be preached to them in the power of the Spirit. For Lydia to enter the kingdom, Jesus' representatives had to go to Philippi to tell her and others the message of the kingdom. The Acts of the Apostles, which describes the first comings of the kingdom with power in people's lives, ends in Rome with Paul preaching the kingdom of God and teaching about the Lord Jesus Christ. 'From morning till evening he explained and declared to them the kingdom of God and tried to convince them about Jesus from the Law of Moses and from the Prophets' (Acts 28:23). 'Boldly and without hindrance he preached the kingdom of God and taught about the Lord Jesus Christ' (Acts 28:31). That is how the kingdom comes now in human lives in preparation for the coming Kingdom.

All Christians represent their King. The apostles knew themselves to be 'Christ's ambassadors', and Christians are to see themselves as the Lord Jesus Christ's representatives in the world. God makes his appeal to men and women through us. We implore them 'on Christ's behalf: Be reconciled to God' (2 Corinthians 5:20), because of the atoning sacrifice for sin God has provided in his Son (2 Corinthians 5:21; 1 John 2:2). As the Father sent his Son, so the Son sends his representatives (John 20:21).

By proclaiming the gospel to men and women we are privileged 'to open their eyes and turn them from darkness to light, and from the power of Satan to God, so that they may receive forgiveness of sins and a place among those who are sanctified by faith' in Christ (Acts 26:18). Knowing 'what it is to fear the Lord, we try to persuade men' (2 Corinthians 5:11). 'As God's fellow-workers we urge' men and women 'not to receive God's grace in vain' (2 Corinthians 6:1). When people listen to our Lord Jesus Christ's ambassadors, they, in effect, listen to him; and when they reject them, they reject him (Luke 10:16).

For some of us, representing the King will mean being sent to preach the kingdom of God away from where we now live (Luke 9:2,60), leaving home, family and friends for the kingdom of God's sake (Luke 18:29). But the responsibility of being servants of the King does not rest upon the few who are called to uproot themselves from home and family. We are all to be 'fellow-workers for the kingdom of God' (Colossians 4:11), as we actively support evangelistic and missionary work, and as we ourselves tell others the good news about Jesus, our Saviour and King. A worthy watchword of the early Inter Varsity Missionary Fellowship was 'Evangelise to a finish to bring back the King.'

God's kingdom requires committed service - service that is sustained throughout the whole of life. It may involve great cost, many hardships (Acts 14:22) and even suffering (2 Thessalonians 1:5). The apostle John links the kingdom with suffering and patient endurance (Revelation 1:9), implying that of necessity they belong together. But have we cause to complain? Is that not the path our King trod before us? In praying, 'Your Kingdom come,' we place our lives at our King's disposal.

LOYAL CITIZENS

Loyal citizens is the third picture the Lord's Prayer provides of what it means to be a Christian. With John Newton we can sing,

Saviour, if of Zion's city
I through grace a member am,
Let the world deride or pity,

> *I will glory in thy Name:*
> *Fading is the worldling's pleasure,*
> *All his boasted pomp and show;*
> *Solid joys and lasting treasure*
> *None but Zion's children know.*

Our true citizenship is already in heaven 'and we eagerly await a Saviour from there, the Lord Jesus Christ, who, by the power that enables him to bring everything under his control, will transform our lowly bodies so that they will be like his glorious body' (Philippians 3:20,21).

Chapter 4

Obedient servants

'Your will be done on earth as it is in heaven'

The expression 'God willing' sums up an attitude to life the Bible encourages, especially when we make plans (James 4:13-15). The apostle Paul planned his programme with the proviso, 'If the Lord permits' (1 Corinthians 16:7). That is not to say that we must pepper our conversation with liberal helpings of the phrase 'If it is the Lord's will' or that we should put D.V. - the initials representing the Latin words Deo Violente ('the Lord willing') - on all invitations to meetings and special occasions. More important than the words or initials is the conviction in our hearts that in all our plans we are dependent upon God and subject to his will. We change our minds often because things turn out differently from what we expect and we cannot see into the future. But not so with God: like his understanding, wisdom and power, his will is eternal and unchanging.

GOD'S WILL DOES NOT CHANGE

Whatever God wills or decrees is hard and fast, totally permanent; whatever he promises, he carries out. He declares of his Word, 'It will not return to me empty, but will accomplish what I desire and achieve the purpose for which I sent it' (Isaiah 55:11). 'What I have said, that will I bring about; what I have planned, that will I do' (Isaiah 46:11). 'God is not a man, that he should lie, nor a son of man, that he should change his mind. Does he speak and then not act? Does he promise and not fulfil?' (Numbers 23:19) There cannot be any reason for change in God's will. Having infinite understanding, he knows all future events. Nothing happens without either his permission or direction. No intelligence is superior to his; no event is unforeseen by him; no unrighteousness is found in him; and no power is equal to his.

During a visit to Zimbabwe for a conference of military chaplains, I needed to get back from Keriba (where the famous dam is) to Harare, but bad weather put an aircraft in the wrong place and there was no flight at the expected time. But just as I was about to undertake the journey by van instead, I - with three others - was offered the opportunity to travel in a six-seater aircraft. If you wonder who occupied the sixth seat, it was a crate of fish, next to which I was seated in the back because I was the smallest! It was a fascinating experience because we flew at a much lower height and slower speed than the aircraft that had brought me there. Sometimes we followed the course of a river or more often the route of the main highway. Down below I could see the cars on the main road below, travelling in both directions. From my higher vantage point I could see the towns and villages from which they had come some time before, and the places to which they were travelling. It was different for the drivers of the cars below: they could see only up to the next bend in the road or as far as their limited vision allowed. Looking in both directions, I could see where two cars were going to meet, perhaps unexpectedly so far as they were concerned, as they came to a twist in the road. I saw in this experience a picture of God's knowledge. Our Father sees the beginning and end of the whole of our journey, and all the twists of the road in between. He knows all that is ahead of us, both in the immediate and the future.

God's is a sovereign will. As Creator, he has dominion over all his creatures. There is none to whom he has to answer for his actions; and all he does is good. God's knowledge means that he knows the correct outcome for everything; and his wisdom directs everything to the best end. God is perfectly, perpetually and incomparably wise.

GOD'S WILL IS DONE IN HEAVEN

In heaven God's rule and reign are acknowledged. There angels and the redeemed rejoice in his kingship and delight to please him. Obedience to God's will is the angels' joy. They are his 'mighty ones who do his bidding, who obey his word' (Psalm 103:20). The angels do God's will regularly, sincerely, willingly, enthusiastically, swiftly and perfectly.

Jews express the angels' obedience in a prayer in their daily morning service: 'Your name be magnified for ever, our King and Creator of many servants, who stand in the higher worlds, and who proclaim aloud, with reverence, the commands of the living God. They are all of them lovely, chosen, and mighty; they all obey with fear the command of their Creator: they all open their mouths, in holiness and purity, in song and in praise, to bless, and hallow, and magnify, and extol the name of the Omnipotent. ... All of them, in various gradations, perform the duties of the heavenly kingdom, and encourage one another to praise the Lord with holy delight - in pure language and melody, in harmony and reverence, sounds the ascription of holiness, Holy, holy, holy, Lord God of Hosts, the fulness of all the earth is his majesty.'

In heaven God's saints who have gone before us 'serve him day and night' (Revelation 7:15). Heaven is not a place of holy inactivity, but of joyful obedience to God. In this petition we are praying that here on earth we may do what 'the spirits of righteous men made perfect' (Hebrews 12:23) do, together with 'all his heavenly host' - 'his servants who do his will' (Psalm 103:21).

TWO ASPECTS OF GOD'S WILL

God's will is hidden unless he chooses to reveal it to us (Ephesians 1:9). His thoughts are not our thoughts, neither are his ways our ways (Isaiah 55:8). Two aspects of God's will may be distinguished. First, there is his inscrutable (secret) or hidden will, through which his purposes in the world and universe are carried out. The Bible word often associated with God's will is 'mystery'. The Bible uses it for a divine secret hitherto concealed, but now revealed. The best example is the coming into the world of our Lord Jesus - his Incarnation and death on the Cross. The Incarnation, and the Cross which was its purpose, summed up God's will for the achievement of the salvation of men and women. The great 'mystery' of God's will - the truth the gospel reveals - is how he brings men and women back into a right relationship with himself. It was God's will from the beginning, and it was hinted at and promised in the Old Testament, but it became clear only with our Saviour's coming. It is only because God has chosen to reveal this 'mystery' that we can understand it.

It is part of God's hidden will, for example, that God chose Christians in Christ 'before the creation of the world to be holy and blameless in his sight. In love he predestined us to be adopted as his sons through Jesus Christ, in accordance with his pleasure and will' (Ephesians 1:4,5). That act of election has nothing to do with human achievements, good or bad, but is entirely a matter of God's will (Romans 9:11), that is, God's secret and hidden will. We do not understand God's choice, and we cannot say beforehand whom he has chosen. Such sovereign acts are not open to our inspection.

Secondly, there is God's declared or visible will, which is written down in the Bible. We are duty bound to search out and know his will as it is found here, because the Bible has been given for this purpose. God does tell us, for example, that, although we cannot see how he is working out his purposes in the world, the climax will be the unifying of everything, and his heading them up in our Lord Jesus Christ (Ephesians 1:10). As a consequence of sin the whole of creation was brought into disorder. But through the Lord Jesus everything will be restored to its proper function and unity. The entire creation will find its one Head in our Lord Jesus Christ. When we pray, 'Your will be done on earth as it is in heaven,' we are asking God that this, his declared goal, will soon be achieved.

The Bible also teaches us on a very practical level what we are to avoid and what we are to pursue: it discloses God's will for our daily life. We are to grasp firmly what his revealed will is (Ephesians 5:17). Dr. Karl Kumm, one of the first four missionaries of the Sudan United Mission, often quoted Albert, the Prince Consort, 'Gentlemen, find out the will of God for your day and generation and then, as quickly as possible, get into line ...' It is observable that those who make most of the Scriptures make most progress in the Christian life.

GOD'S WILL AND GOD'S WORD

Our preoccupation, therefore, must not be with God's secret or hidden will, but with his disclosed will. This underlines the importance of the Bible. Able to make us wise for salvation through faith in our Lord Jesus

Christ, all Scripture, being 'God-breathed' 'is useful for teaching, rebuking, correcting and training in righteousness,' so that we 'may be thoroughly equipped for every good work' (2 Timothy 3:15-17). Jottings Warren Wiersbe, an American Bible teacher, found in an old Bible Study Book in a library put it well: 'All Scripture is given by inspiration of God and is profitable for:

doctrine - what is right;

reproof - what is not right;

correction - how to get right;

instruction in righteousness - how to keep right.'

Genuine faith in the truth of God's Word is crucial to a life of obedience to God's will. As Great-Heart says in John Bunyan's *The Pilgrim's Progress:*

> *The Bible! That's the book, the book indeed,*
> *The book of books!*
> *On which who looks,*
> *As he should do aright, shall never need*
> *Wish for another light*
> *To guide him in the night.*

Nothing is more encouraging to those who teach and preach God's Word than to find their hearers following with their Bibles in their hands. Any school without text-books is in a sorry state, and the one text book of the Church, the School of Christ, is the Bible. During the New York Revival of 1858 a converted sea captain asked for permission to say a few words in a meeting. Speaking with great conviction he said, 'See what we have! We have a book of directions; we have a compass; we have a chart; we have all the rocks and shoals laid down; we have our course laid straight to heaven. No sailor was ever half so well provided. He must be a poor sea captain that cannot get his vessel into port.'

The Bible declares God's will in order that it may be obeyed - 'done' - in our lives. As Calvin put it, the Scriptures 'provide us with spectacles through which to interpret the world and to live it for God's glory.' Andrew MacBeath was a greatly loved Principal of the Bible Training Institute in Glasgow (now the Glasgow Bible College). Soon after his appointment, he 'was shown a copy of the prospectus. He told the Board he wished to change one sentence. What was that? The sentence declared that "students should accept the Bible as the supreme authority in all matters of faith and practice." Silence! "Yes," he said, "it should read, 'students should accept **and use** the Bible as the supreme authority in all matters of faith and practice'."' The members of the Board uttered a sigh of relief! What is declared in Scripture to be pleasing to God is be to translated by obedience into daily conduct. As Martin Luther, the sixteenth century reformer, put it, 'To obey God is better than to work miracles.' God teaches us his ways so that we may walk in them (Isaiah 2:3).

Our Lord Jesus often repeated fundamental truths and the gospels report them in ways that serve to interpret them. So, for instance, Matthew and Mark record Jesus' words, 'For whoever does the will of my Father in heaven is my brother and sister and mother' (Matthew 12:50; cf. Mark 3:35). In Luke, however, our Lord says, 'My mother and brothers are those who hear God's word and put it into practice' (Luke 8:21). The one statement interprets the other: God's will is God's Word. Nothing may be said to be God's will which contradicts his Word.

GOD'S DECLARED WILL

God's declared will is the salvation of men and women. Salvation is not his occasional act - we could almost say that it is one of his attributes. He is 'the saving God'. He 'wants all men to be saved and to come to a knowledge of the truth. For there is one God and one mediator between God and men, the man Christ Jesus' (1 Timothy 2:4,5). The context of this statement makes plain that it does not have in view all men and women individually, but men and women without regard to their position in society, or their race or nationality. We may be tempted to want to raise here the question of election. But that has to do with God's inscrutable or hidden will, and we are not to concern ourselves with things which God has not chosen to make plain. But these words do reveal that God calls all men and women to a knowledge of the truth, and he has their salvation at heart. We know that God has promised his Son an inheritance from among all the nations (Psalm 2:8), and that the gospel is God's power for the salvation of everyone who believes (Romans 1:16).

The best Bible commentary is the Bible itself. We see God's will in action in our Lord Jesus. He came down from heaven not to do his own will but the will of the Father who sent him (John 6:38). We know from the gospels that the Lord Jesus delighted to invite all men and women to come to him (Matthew 11:28-30), with the confidence that all that the Father had given him would - and will - come to him (John 6:37). There is an inherent mystery about this which we cannot unravel. On the one hand God does not convert men and women to himself against their will; he never forces anyone to receive his Son. Yet, on the other hand, he conquers the will and it becomes obedient - such is the power of grace. The security of believers is sure. 'And this is the will of him who sent me, that I shall lose none of all that he has given me, but raise them up at the last day. For my Father's will is that everyone who looks to the Son and believes in him shall have eternal life, and I will raise him up at the last day' (John 6:39-40). It is not the Father's will that the Son should lose any given to him. We are encouraged to pray in this petition, therefore, for the salvation of men and women. A basic rule of prayer is that our prayers should be guided and regulated by what we clearly know to be God's will.

Samuel Prime's account of the revival in New York in 1858 - entitled *The Power of Prayer* - describes how seven praying women, all of whom had unconverted husbands, met specifically for prayer for the conversion of their partners. They prayed for ten years, and received no positive answers to their prayers. Then some were for giving up, discouraged and disheartened. An Irish woman, though poor and uneducated, was not spiritually so. She said, "We must not give up our meeting. Do you know that God is faithful to all his promises? He has never said, 'Seek ye me in vain.'" 'So they prayed on three years more, and all their children were converted, their husbands were converted, the Lord poured out his Spirit in great power, and their friends and neighbours were converted, the church received large accessions, and the Lord turned almost the whole people to himself.'

God's declared will, after our new birth, is our sanctification. Sanctification flows from justification. God never pardons sinners without going on to sanctify them. He receives us as we are, but he does not leave us as we are! It is part and parcel of the good work he begins in us which he will carry on to completion until the day of our Lord Jesus Christ's return (Philippians 1:6).

Sanctification is often a painful process. C. S. Lewis likened it to going to the dentist. He remembered how as a boy he often had toothache, but he did not go to his mother to get something to deaden the pain. His reason was simple: he knew that while she would give him something right away, the next morning she would take him to the dentist! 'I wanted immediate relief from pain: but I couldn't get it without having my teeth set permanently right. And I knew these dentists; I knew they started fiddling about with all sorts of other teeth which hadn't yet begun to ache. They wouldn't let sleeping dogs lie.' He then went on to liken the Lord to the dentist in that if once we call him in, 'he will give you the full treatment.'

God's will that we should be holy is most relevant and practical. For example, it demands the avoidance of sexual immorality in all its forms, and our learning to control our own bodies in a way that is pure and treats them with respect (1 Thessalonians 4:3-5). New birth changes our attitudes in this area of life. God's grace teaches us to root the wrong things out by his strength. The word 'learning' is important. Grace does not complete its work in a day.

Expressed another way, God's will is that we should live righteous lives (James 1:20). Righteousness is holiness expressed in moral principles (Isaiah 5:16). Right with God, we find we want to do what is right. New birth is a new birth to righteousness (1 John 2:29). God's purpose is that we might be 'filled with the fruit of righteousness' (Philippians 1:11). The Ten Commandments show the obedience God requires; and the Beatitudes the character he wants us to display. Our Lord Jesus 'bore our sins in his body on the tree, so that we might die to sins and live for righteousness' (1 Peter 2:24). Our being right with God - a gift of his justifying grace in the Lord Jesus - brings the responsibility of striving after all that is right in every part of life. There are good works - righteous deeds - which God has planned for us to do (Ephesians 2:10). Christians are to be 'glued' to what is good (Romans 12:9). John Wesley had it right: 'Do all the good you can, by all means that you can, in all ways that you can, at all times that you can, to all people that you can, for as long as you can.' Good works are the fruit and proof of faith (Luke 6:43-49). Goodness has as its objects, not just those who do us good, but those who may even be our enemies (Luke 6:27,28).

A further aspect of our sanctification is that we should give ourselves first to God and then to one another (2 Corinthians 8:5). We are not simply to pray that this may be the case, but we are to do it! Sin is primarily self-centredness, and sanctification gets to work here. Self is one of the toughest weeds that grows in the garden of life, and God helps us to deal with it by giving us glimpses of our self and the areas in which we need to change. Sometimes he gives us a fresh view of the sinfulness of our own hearts, which apart from his grace might drive us to despair. Instead of wanting to live for self, we want to give ourselves to him and to others. We cannot set a limit to where such self-giving ends. Our God-given spiritual gifts are not to be used for personal or selfish pleasure but for the good of others - they are gifts for the body of Christ. Significantly, the giving of ourselves to God, as we ought in view of his mercy in the Lord Jesus, is a secret of our personal discovery of his will (Romans 12:1,2).

Sanctification is the process of which holiness is the completed state. In sanctification, God's will is that sinful attitudes and actions should be put to death in our life, our nature and character renewed after the image of God in Christ, and our obedience to God increased so that we live to please God. Sanctification is the continual endeavour to bring holiness to completion (2 Corinthians 7:1). It is a progressive work and involves our complete personality: our spirit, soul and body (1 Thessalonians 5:23). Our entire sanctification will not be realised until our bodies are changed to be like our Lord Jesus Christ's body (Philippians 3:21; 1 John 3:2). All these things take place through the power of the Holy Spirit. By the help of the Holy Spirit who lives within us, we are enabled to keep under control, although not eradicate, what the Bible calls 'our old self', and to suppress, although not put an end to, our sinful desires. We are enabled to resist the world, the flesh and the devil, and to grow in grace, not suddenly, but day by day until our life's end or the return of our Lord Jesus.

Augustine spoke of the battle that goes on continuously in our lives. 'My thoughts, and the deepest places of my soul are torn with every kind of tumult until the day when I shall be purified and melted in the fire of your love, and wholly joined to you.' Sanctification is, in effect, spiritual growth. It is therefore a continuous process, so that we can say with John Newton, 'I am not what I ought to be, I am not what I want to be, I am not what I hope to be in another world, but still I am not what I once used to be, and by the grace of God I am what I am.' As sanctification proceeds, our attitudes and actions change for the good, often in ways which we may not recognise because increasingly they become unconscious reflexes.

Exhortations like, 'Be joyful always; pray continually; give thanks in all circumstances, for this is God's will for you in Christ Jesus' (1 Thessalonians 5:16-18) indicate that holiness is happiness. God's will done in our lives is a secret of unique joy. Satan does all he can to misrepresent holiness. He suggests that it is narrow, restricting and confining, a source of misery and devoid of joy, whereas the truth is that it is the opposite. He would even make Christians ashamed of it if he possibly can. John Wesley warned one of his closest friends, Ebenezer Blackwell, a banker, against 'being ashamed, not of sin, but of holiness.' I have kept by me for some time words I found quoted from an anonymous source in an eighteenth century writer:

> Lord, be thy pleasure always mine;
> I wish to have no will but thine;
> This, this is heav'n enough for me
> Quite to be swallowed up in thee.

COMMON ASPECTS OF GOD'S WILL

God's will extends to the small details of life: to our function in the body of Christ, to our daily employment, to our state in life - married or unmarried, with or without children - to our physical and material well-being, and much else besides.

Whatever gifts or functions we have in the church, they are determined according to God's choice (1 Corinthians 12:4-6); he distributes them according to his will (Hebrews 2:4). The gifts of the Spirit are part of the gifts of the ascended Lord Jesus to his Church: 'To each one of us grace has been given as Christ apportioned it' (Ephesians 4:7). Hence Paul could write, 'Paul, an apostle of Christ Jesus by the will of God' (2 Corinthians 1:1), and address Archippus, whose function in the church is not disclosed, 'See to it that you complete the work you have received in the Lord' (Colossians 4:17)

To be married is God's gift to some (1 Corinthians 7:7), and to be unmarried is his equal gift to others (1 Corinthians 7:17). Children likewise are God's gift and the withholding of that gift is also in his providence. The experience of Abraham and Sarah (Genesis 17:15-22), Hannah and Elkanah (1 Samuel 1) and Zechariah and Elizabeth testifies to this (Luke 1:5-25).

God's will may include physical suffering and pain. Losing his most precious relationships and possessions, Job declared, 'The LORD gave and the LORD has taken away; may the name of the LORD be praised' (Job 1:21). God is always in control of our sufferings, much as circumstances may seem to argue differently (Psalm 34:20). General Booth, the founder of the Salvation Army, lost the sight of one eye, and his second eye was operated on for cataract but without success. His son was entrusted with the responsibility of telling his father that the specialist had pronounced him blind. After the truth had been told him, the General's first words were, 'I shall never see your face again?' Then after a moment, he calmly said, 'God must know best.' After a pause, he continued, 'I have done what I could for God and the people with my eyes. Now I shall do what I can for God and the people without my eyes.'

Opposition and persecution are likewise within God's will for some (1 Peter 4:19). The Lord Jesus warned that our relationship to him may bring hatred, exclusion, insult and rejection at the hands of the world

(Luke 6:22). 'If the world hates you, keep in mind that it hated me first. If you belonged to the world, it would love you as its own. As it is, you do not belong to the world, but I have chosen you out of the world. That is why the world hates you. Remember the words I spoke to you: "No servant is greater than his master." If they persecuted me, they will persecute you also' (John 15:18-20). 'I have told you these things, so that in me you may have peace. In this world you will have trouble. But take heart! I have overcome the world' (John 16:33). Barnabas and Paul 'returned to Lystra, Iconium and Antioch, strengthening the disciples and encouraging them to remain true to the faith. "We must go through many hardships to enter the kingdom of God," they said' (Acts 14:21,22). Trials were the experience of God's faithful people in the Old Testament period (Hebrews 11:32-40). Shadrach, Meshach and Abednego literally experienced a fiery trial (Daniel 3:19ff; 1 Peter 4:12). In prison Paul called himself the Lord's prisoner (e.g. Ephesians 3:1; 2 Timothy 1:8).

Suffering was the Father's will for his Son: 'it was the LORD's will to crush him and cause him to suffer' (Isaiah 53:10). To serve the body of Christ faithfully, frequently involves suffering: we may be called upon to fill up in our 'flesh what is still lacking in regard to Christ's afflictions, for the sake of his body, which is the church' (Colossians 1:24). That does not mean that our afflictions have a place in making a propitiation for sin - our Saviour's work was utterly and finally unique in this. But our sufferings can aid the propagation of the gospel. There is a quota of sufferings which the body of Christ must bear in fulfilment of her Master's commission to preach the gospel faithfully (Colossians 1:24f; cf. Matthew 24:6; Mark 13:8; Luke 21:9). As one of the 16th century reformers, Menno Simons (1496-1561), the founder of the Mennonites, said, 'If the Head had to suffer such torture, anguish, misery, and pain, how shall his servants, children, and members expect peace and freedom as to their flesh?'.

There are times when we actively pursue God's will, working hard at what we know pleases him. But there are also periods when God brings bitter experiences into our lives which we would never choose, and we then have to work hard to please him in them. This submissive or passive obedience may be far more difficult to achieve than active obedience to his will, for God calls us to carry ourselves well in the difficulties - and even the evils - he permits.

AN INEVITABLE QUESTION

Why should we pray 'Your will be done on earth as it is in heaven' when we know that God is sovereign and that his purposes are unchanging?

First, we pray, 'Your will be done' because God tells us to do so! As we have established, his will is in many aspects hidden and secret, and therefore a puzzle to us. But he chooses to give his people's prayers a role in the outworking of his will. Prayer is one of the mysterious wheels in God's providence by which his purposes are executed. If we look inside a conventional watch with its intricate movements, we see wheels going in opposite directions, and it seems incredible that they all work together to achieve their sole purpose of telling the time. We do not have to know how each of the wheels operates to benefit from their functioning. We do not have to understand what prayer does in relation to God's will in order to benefit from his purposes in it.

Secondly, our Lord Jesus Christ himself set an example by praying for the Father's will to be done. His decisions were born of prayer, as he sought the Father's will about the choosing of the twelve apostles (Luke 6:12), and then later he asked them the important question about their understanding of his identity as the Messiah and Son of God (Luke 9:18). In the Garden of Gethsemane, his preoccupation was with doing the Father's will whatever the cost (Luke 22:42); and that will was the passion of his life. He came down from heaven not to do his own will, but his Father's (John 5:30; 6:38). With his Father's law in his heart, his Father's pleasure was his delight (Psalm 40:8; Hebrews 10:5-7). His food was to do his Father's will and to finish his work (John 4:34). Since it was the Father's will to bruise him and put him to death for our sins (Isaiah 53:10), he said 'Yes' even to the Cross.

While our Lord's redeeming work was unique and possible to him alone, the Father calls us to take up our cross also and to follow his Son's example of obedience. The path of obedience varies from disciple to disciple and for some it will be severe and costly. Because God is good as well as sovereign, he delights in willing rather than conscripted obedience. He allows us the privilege of wanting to be eager to do his will. We are free to make any choice we want and God gives us the liberty to choose the second best or worse, instead of the best. But when we understand that his will is 'good, pleasing and perfect' (Romans 12:2), we choose his will even if it is the pathway of the Cross, as our Saviour did.

Thirdly, prayer is a means of aligning our wills with God's. Three times in the Garden of Gethsemane our Lord Jesus prayed the same prayer: 'Father, if you are willing, take this cup from me; yet not my will, but yours be done' (Luke 22:42). Knowing what God's will was did not make it easy to do; praying 'Your will be done' once was not sufficient. But as our Saviour aligned his will with his Father's, at unimaginable cost, so blessing came to us. In prayer our endeavour must be to make our desires coincide with God's will (Romans 1:10). I live in the city of Edinburgh where at one o'clock each afternoon something takes place very predictably. As people walk along its main street, Princes Street, at one o'clock precisely a gun is fired high above them from the castle ramparts. If I am there to hear it I instinctively look at my watch - and I am not alone! I not only look at my watch but I correct it if it is wrong. I do not think for a moment that the gun is wrong because I know it is timed exactly with Big Ben. When we pray aright, our longing, without reservation, is to make our wills coincide with God's will.

We do not destroy our own will in praying 'Your will be done' but we submerge it into God's will. As Tennyson put it, 'Our wills are ours, we know not how; Our wills are ours to make them thine.' In making this request, we affirm that God knows best. A hymn expresses it well -

He always wins who sides with God,
To him no change is lost;
God's will is sweetest to him when
It triumphs at his cost.

Ill that he blesses is our good,
  And unblest good is ill;
And all is right that seems most wrong,
  If it be his sweet Will!

Fourthly, prayer is a means of gaining strength to do God's will. Having prayed 'Your will be done' in the Garden of Gethsemane, Luke records that an angel came and strengthened our Lord Jesus (22:43). That strengthening did not diminish the anguish, but it sustained him in his prayer for God's will to be done (Luke 22:44,45). Our strength is renewed as we look to God (Isaiah 40:31). With David we may pray, 'Teach me to do your will, for you are my God; may your good Spirit lead me on level ground' (Psalm 143:10). God is able to work in us 'to will and to act according to his good purpose' (Philippians 2:13).

We discover that we often encounter God afresh when we set ourselves to do his will. Madame Guyon, the French mystic of the seventeenth and early eighteenth century, found it so: 'Whenever I meet with the will of God, I feel that I meet with God; whenever I respect and love the will of God, I feel that I respect and love God; whenever I unite with the will of God, I feel that I unite with God. So that practically and religiously, although I am aware that a difference can be made philosophically, God and the will of God are to me the same. He who is in perfect harmony with the **will** of God, is as much in harmony with God himself, as it is possible for any being to be. The very name of God's will fills me with joy.' 'I can truly say, that, standing in God's will, and doing and suffering his will, I have something which strengthens, animates, and encourages me; I am fed with a nourishment which the world cannot give.'

A CONSEQUENCE OF NEW BIRTH

This petition must be seen in relation to the preceding requests of the Lord's Prayer. To want to do God's will is a fruit of new birth into God's family. Born again of his Spirit, the Spirit of his Son in us not only cries 'Abba Father!' but also 'Not my will, but Yours be done!' As the godly

English reformer and Bible Translator, William Tyndale (c1494-1536), put it, 'That we desire to follow the will of God, it is the gift of Christ's blood. That we now hate the devil's will (whereunto we were so fast locked, and could not but love it), is also the gift of Christ's blood; unto whom belongeth the praise and honour of our good deeds, and not unto us.' The essence of sonship is obedience, a response to unspeakable love and inexhaustible grace. Obedience is not difficult since God's commands have become his enablings. God calls us to nothing for which he does not provide the power to achieve it (Philippians 2:12,13).

As children of our heavenly Father, we want his Name to be honoured and his kingdom to come; but that can be only as his will is done, and done by us on purpose. It is, therefore, appropriate to ask our Father to fill us 'with the knowledge of his will through all spiritual wisdom and understanding' (Colossians 1:9; cf. Ephesians 5:17). The knowledge of God's will is not said to come through special or immediate revelation, but significantly by 'spiritual wisdom and under-standing'. These latter two qualities underline that there is no short-cut to seeing things from God's viewpoint. They are given by the Holy Spirit through a deep, accurate and comprehensive acquaintance with the Scriptures. God's great design in giving us his Word is to make us doers of his will. His Spirit opens our minds to understand his Word and its application to life. But any prayer to **know** God's will must be accompanied by the desire to **do** it. God delights to provide us with every good thing we need in order to do his will (Hebrews 13:21).

CHECKING OUR AGENDA

Since we have every confidence concerning the perfection of our Father's hidden and inscrutable will, it is our delight to pray that his will may be done, and that the day of our Saviour's return may be hastened - we have to use human language (2 Peter 3:12) - so that we may see everything brought together under one head, even our Lord Jesus Christ (Ephesians 1:10), and God seen to be wholly and absolutely God (1 Corinthians 15:28).

But God's declared or disclosed will, which the Bible makes known, must be our principal concern when we pray, 'Your will be done on earth as it is in heaven'. Important questions follow. Is the salvation of men and women on our prayer agenda? Is our personal sanctification there too? Are all our plans submitted to God? Do we deliberately, and daily, align our wills with his as we pray?

OBEDIENT SERVANTS

Obedient servants is the fourth picture the Lord's Prayer provides of what it means to be a Christian. We are to be obedient servants, always praying, 'Your will be done on earth as it is in heaven.' While we are sons and daughters, we delight to call ourselves God's servants, having the mind and attitude of his Son Jesus Christ (Philippians 2:5ff). His service is our delight; and his will our greatest pleasure.

Chapter 5

Unashamed dependants

'Give us today our daily bread'

Though the first three petitions of the Lord's Prayer have priority over those that follow, the latter are not to be considered as at all unimportant. The first three concern God and the preoccupation we should have with his interests. The remaining petitions have to do with our personal needs. The honour of God's Name must be put before any anxiety for our own reputation, the interest of his kingdom before any personal interest, and his will must have precedence over our every desire.

This division teaches an important lesson and principle. As a general rule it is appropriate in our prayers to begin with God's concerns. His affairs are more important than ours, and the more concerned we are for the honour of his Name, the coming of his kingdom, and the doing of his will, the more his interests will take precedence. But the principle of beginning with God's concerns is not to be followed ruthlessly and coldly. There are times when our personal need - or that of others - is urgent. So too should our cry be, as was David's: 'Come quickly to help me, O Lord my Saviour' (Psalm 38:22). On other occasions it may not be so much personal petitions that flood our minds, but rather our sense of unworthiness, so well expressed by John Newton in one of his hymns:

With my burden I begin;
Lord, remove this load of sin!
Let thy blood for sinners spilt
Set my conscience free from guilt.

There has been a tendency to spiritualize this petition, and to think, for example, of the bread of the Lord's Supper, the spiritual food of the Word of God, or the Lord Jesus Christ himself, the Bread of Life.

Helpful as such thoughts may be, they are not what these words have in view.

If this petition were not here, we might think it presumptuous or impudent to include it, and especially to put it first in our list of personal requirements. But our heavenly Father knows our needs and delights to supply them. Our practical, material and personal concerns matter to him. We are not to hide them because he delights in our sharing them with him and expressing our dependence upon him.

With good reason we are encouraged to pray about our basic physical and material requirements: the God who has become our Heavenly Father is the Maker of all things. He conceives, sustains, looks after and directs everything to its intended end. The Book of Psalms, which has much to say about God's provision for his children, also focuses much upon his creative activity (e.g. Psalms 19 and 100, to mention but two). I like John Calvin's description of the world around us as a 'theatre of God's glory' and the thought that 'the psalmists have season tickets in this theatre.' When God created seed-bearing plants and fruit-producing trees, his purpose was the provision of food for men and women and others of his creatures: 'He makes grass grow for the cattle, and plants for man to cultivate - bringing forth food from the earth: wine that gladdens the heart of man, oil to make his face shine, and bread that sustains his heart' (Psalm 104:14,15; cf. Genesis 1:29,30) We see a distinction here between ourselves and all other creatures: we have the ability to cultivate plants, to make bread and wine from the fruits of the earth; whereas the cattle, for example, eat what is there, as it is. But the one Provider is God, and he is the source of all the fruits of the earth, and of the intelligence given to use the fruits he provides: he gives food to every creature, providing 'seed for the sower and bread for the eater' (Isaiah 55:10; 2 Corinthians 9:10). With food there goes the provision of clothing (Deuteronomy 10:18).

Not only will our Heavenly Father provide what we need, but what is best for us. It is not perhaps easy to accept at first, but some of us cannot handle either wealth or poverty as well as others. Wealth can spoil us, whereas others may rise to the opportunity of being first class stewards of it for the benefit of other people, and especially God's family. The prosperity that others find easy to handle, we might find perilous. The writer of Proverbs knew this: 'Give me neither poverty nor riches, but give me only my daily bread. Otherwise, I may have too much and disown you and say, "Who is the LORD?" Or I may become poor and steal, and so dishonour the name of my God' (Proverbs 30:8,9). There is a danger of our asking for material benefits which God in his love and wisdom denies us because our motivation is basically - and sometimes entirely - selfish, and which if he granted would lead us further astray (James 4:3). God is the Giver of 'every good and perfect gift' (James 1:17). We often fail to look beyond the gifts to the Giver. This prayer encourages us to fix our eyes where they ought to be.

New birth opens our eyes not only to our Creator but also to his creation. It is as if suddenly the whole of creation becomes a mighty pipe organ and God's breath blows through all its pipes. Illumined by the Spirit and using the spectacles of Scripture, we appreciate the world around us as never before. Christians in every period of history have found this so.

Jonathan Edwards (1703-1758) described one of the consequences of his conversion in these terms: 'The appearance of everything was altered; there seemed to be, as it were, a calm ... appearance of divine glory, in almost every thing. God's excellency, his wisdom, his purity and love, seemed to appear in every thing: in the sun, moon, and stars; in the clouds, and blue sky; in the grass, flowers, trees; in the water, and all nature; which used greatly to fix in my mind.'

Under conviction of sin, a husband told his believing wife and they kneeled down to pray. 'After she had prayed, he attempted to pray, and all he could say was, "God be merciful to me a sinner." This he repeated more than fifty times! He could not go to sleep that night, but continued to weep and pray; hearing the clock strike and tick till near morning. Every tick of the clock seemed to say, "Jesus lives! Jesus lives!" Suddenly he found himself walking the room in an ecstasy of delight - and, as he looked out of the window, such beauty never met his eyes before. He longed for the morning to come, so that he might tell of his Saviour, and how he had found him, and what a blessedness there was in believing in him.'

Abraham Vereide, the instigator of the annual Presidential Prayer Breakfasts in the USA, described how at his conversion he threw himself to the ground to cry his heart out to God. As he prayed, he had a vivid awareness of God's presence, and words of Scripture gave him assurance of salvation. He said, 'I rose to my feet, and as I looked around, everything seemed to be so beautiful, the moss, the grass, the trees, the leaves, the sky above me, everything had taken on a different hue.' The experience of Billy Bray, the nineteenth century evangelist, was similar, 'Everything looked new to me, the people, the fields, the cattle, the trees. I was like a man in a new world.' From our hearts we can sing,

> *Heaven above is softer blue,*
> *Earth around is sweeter green;*
> *Something lives in every hue*
> *Christless eyes have never seen.*

THE SYMBOLIC NATURE OF BREAD

Bread sums up our basic material needs. It stands for all the daily benefits we require such as food and clothing, housing and heating, and so forth. We are asking here for life's necessities. Most communities and societies have a staple diet which may be described as their 'bread'. Having eaten food and also shared in the Lord's Supper in different parts of Europe and of Africa, the Far East, and of North and South America, I have been made aware of the variety of forms bread takes. Bread represents what is fundamental to human survival, and which all require to sustain life. For the Jews, like many other peoples, bread was their basic food. 'To eat bread' was 'to have a meal'.

The Bible provides illustrations of bread as the vital commodity for life. When Abraham, prior to the destruction of Sodom and Gomorrah, received heavenly visitors, he instructed Sarah, 'Quick, get three seahs of fine flour and knead it and bake some bread' (Genesis 18:6). When Esau was desperate for food, Jacob gave him 'some bread and some lentil stew' (Genesis 25:34). The complaint of the people when they came out of Egypt into the desert was, 'There is no bread!' (Numbers 21:5). A prosperous land is described as one 'where bread will not be scarce and you will lack nothing' (Deuteronomy 8:9). When Jesus expressed concern for the satisfying of the physical hunger of the crowds listening to him, the disciples asked, 'Where could we get enough bread in this remote place to feed such a crowd?' (Matthew 15:33).

Bread is so basic in the Bible that to eat bread with someone symbolizes intimate fellowship (Exodus 18:12). The Jews, like the Bedouin Arabs today, would have felt it inconceivable to betray someone with whom they had eaten bread and salt. Part of the tragedy of Judas' betrayal was that someone who ate bread with the Saviour should have then gone out and sold him for money (Psalm 41:9; Mark 14:20).

THE BREAD - THE MANNA - IN THE DESERT

Nothing points to bread's essential nature more than God's provision of it for the people of Israel during their forty years in the desert.

The bread - called 'manna' (literally, 'What is it?') - was 'white like coriander seed and tasted like wafers made with honey' (Exodus 16:31). If we ask, 'How were the Israelites sustained for such a long period of time?' the answer is, 'Principally by the provision of bread'. God's promise was, 'I will rain down bread from heaven for you. The people are to go out each day and gather enough for that day' (Exodus 16:4). The purpose behind the daily character of the provision was to test the people to see if they would live in obedience to God: 'In this way I will test them,' God said, 'and see whether they will follow my instructions' (Exodus 16:4).

The bread God gave was to be eaten on the day it was given and was not to be carried over to the next day, except on the day before the Sabbath. Those who tried to keep it discovered that God's provision then bred worms and smelt rotten (Exodus 16:20). On the sixth day the quantity was twice as much as on the previous day, as an extra supply for the Sabbath (Exodus 16:5). Some went out to seek the manna on the Sabbath and found none (Exodus 16:27). God's provision was both wonderful and mysterious: it did not matter how much the people sought to collect on any day, what they gathered was identical (Exodus 16:17,18).

God's provision of bread from heaven lasted forty years until the people came to the habitable land of Canaan and fed upon the food it produced (Exodus 16:35). 'The manna stopped the day after they ate this food from the land; there was no longer any manna for the Israelites, but that year they ate of the produce of Canaan' (Joshua 5:12).

So important a lesson concerning God's provision was it that an omer of the bread was kept and placed before the Lord in front of the Testimony in the Tabernacle (Exodus 16:33,34; Hebrews 9:4).

The manna - the bread from heaven - taught lessons of daily dependence upon God, the sanctity of one day in seven for God (the Sabbath principle), and the sinfulness of selfish hoarding. The overall lesson was to teach them - and us - that 'man does not live on bread alone but on every word that comes from the mouth of the LORD' (Deuteronomy 8:3). We are to trust not in the provision but in the Provider.

ELIJAH

The prophet Elijah too had to learn the lesson of dependence upon God for daily bread. He first appeared on the scene in Israel's history at a time of predicted famine through drought, when he was told by the Lord, 'Hide in the Kerish Ravine, east of the Jordan. You will drink from the brook, and I have ordered the ravens to feed you there' (1 Kings 17:3,4). In the place of obedience God's provision was to be found. And so it was that 'the ravens brought him bread and meat in the evening, and he drank from the brook' (1 Kings 17:6). Once again the food was there a day at a time, calling for a daily dependence upon God.

Then when the brook dried up some time later because of the absence of rain, God provided for Elijah in another way. He instructed him to make his way to Zarephath. 'When he came to the town gate, a widow was there gathering sticks. He called to her and asked, "Would you bring me a little water in a jar so I may have a drink?" As she was going to get it, he called, "And bring me, please, a piece of bread." "As surely as the LORD your God lives," she replied, "I don't have any bread - only a handful of flour in a jar and a little oil in a jug. I am gathering a few sticks to take home and make a meal for myself and my son, that we may eat it - and die." Elijah said to her, "Don't be afraid. Go home and do as you have said. But first make a small cake of bread for me from what you have and bring it to me, and then make something for yourself and your son. For this is what the LORD, the God of Israel says: 'The jar of flour will not be used up and the jug of oil will not run dry until the day the LORD gives rain on the land.' " ' The woman responded in obedience, and every day there was bread for Elijah, and for the woman and her family (1 Kings 17:10-16). God's daily provision fostered Elijah's conscious dependence upon him, and his testimony to God's fatherly care.

Even when Elijah fled to Horeb in a fit of depression after confronting the prophets of Baal on Carmel, and had told the Lord, 'I have had enough, LORD. Take my life; I am no better than my ancestors' (1 Kings 19:4), he found as he awoke from sleep that 'there by his head was a cake of bread baked over hot coals and a jar of water' (1 Kings 19:6).

INNUMERABLE WITNESSES

Elijah's experience of God's provision has been daily multiplied in the life of his people. In 1988 **The Soldiers' and Airmen's Scripture Readers Association** celebrated 150 years of Forces evangelism, and its history entitled *Sovereign Service* records the experience of an early Army Scripture Reader, an ex-Gordon Highlander, who was sent out in 1884 at very short notice to go with the troops proceeding up the Nile to relieve Khartoum. He was then drafted to a hospital where men were pouring in with terrible wounds. 'A few weeks later his unit moved on, and he insisted, despite the hardships, on going with them. By this time he was very short of money as his pay and allowances from head-quarters had not reached him. When he was down to rock-bottom, a Scottish soldier suddenly said: "Got any money?" "Er, - yes," was the reply (after all he still had one piastre!) "Well, take this," said the soldier, holding out some coins. "The Lord told me to give you some money." When asked when it could be repaid, he said: "It's all right, mon; the Lord will see to that." They never met again, but the money lasted till his funds came through.' There is an unmistakeable connection between 'Your will be done' and 'Give us today our daily bread': when we obey God, then he provides for us (Genesis 22:14).

A CONTEMPORARY DEFICIENCY

Living in such a commercial and industrial world, we are inclined to overlook the Giver of our daily bread and to forget our dependence upon him.

A Polish classic entitled *The Outpost* by Aleksander Glowacki, depicts life in rural areas in Europe before our technological revolution. Life on a farm in Poland is described purely and simply in terms of obtaining daily bread: 'All the labour, anxiety, and hopes of these human beings centred in the one aim: daily bread. For this the girl carried in the firewood, or, singing and jumping, ran to the pit for potatoes. For this' the mistress of the holding 'milked the cows at daybreak, baked bread, and moved her saucepans on and off the fire. For this' the smallholder's disabled help 'perspiring, dragged his lame leg after the plough and harrow, and' the master 'murmuring his morning-prayers, went at dawn to the manor-barn or drove into the town to deliver the corn which he had sold to the Jews.' That is a far cry from our going to the supermarket, turning on the electricity or gas or the micro-wave to cook by, or emptying corn-flakes into our plate. But our dependence on God is the same, much as we may lose sight of it.

Coping with affluence rather than with acute need is more our problem. As God warned Israel, 'You may say to yourself, "My power and the strength of my hands have produced this wealth for me." But remember the LORD your God, for it is he who gives you ability to produce wealth' (Deuteronomy 8:17,18). Our success in obtaining the necessities of life is not due to our skill and wisdom alone, but to God's kind provision. When Jacob met his brother Esau after many years, Esau saw the women and children, and the gifts Jacob brought. 'Who are these with you?' he asked. Jacob wisely replied, 'They are the children God has graciously given your servant.' When Esau declared he did not need Jacob's material gifts, Jacob again replied wisely, 'Please accept the present that was brought to you, for God has been gracious to me and I have all I need' (Genesis 33:5-11). Our comparative plenty does not diminish our need to pray 'Give us today our daily bread'; rather it is even more important so that we do not lose sight of our true Provider.

GOD'S PROVISION

God's provision for his children is always good and wise. 'The lions may grow weak and hungry, but those who seek the LORD lack no good thing' (Psalm 34:10). The word 'good' here is important. When God satisfies our desires, he satisfies them 'with good things' (Psalm 103:5; 104:28). As our Lord Jesus put it, 'If you, then, though you are evil, know how to give good gifts to your children, how much more will your Father in heaven give good gifts to those who ask him!' (Matthew 7:11).

God's supply sometimes comes in unexpected ways. Who would have thought that a poor Gentile widow would be God's means of providing bread for Elijah (1 Kings 17:9)? Or that a boy's lunch would produce a meal for five thousand (John 6:1-13)?

GOD'S PROVISION AND DAILY WORK

To depend upon God's provision is not in conflict with earning our daily bread. Rather the Bible encourages us to work hard, but in reliance upon God. Our Lord Jesus himself has given dignity to daily work by his own example as a carpenter in Nazareth. Secular work may be as much a rendering of service to God as the work of those whom we sometimes regard as in 'full-time' service - really a misnomer, since all that every Christian does may be service to God as they do it to please him. Paul and the early missionaries chose not to eat anyone's food without paying for it. On the contrary, they worked night and day, labouring and toiling so that they might not be a burden to any (2 Thessalonians 3:8). Such work in no way opposed the principle of living by faith. Early Christians were urged to settle down and 'earn the bread' that they ate (2 Thessalonians 3:12). Daily work is the means God has ordained for us to obtain our daily bread. 'The labourer's appetite works for him; his hunger drives him on' (Proverbs 16:26). It is a Christian principle that 'If a man will not work' - that is to say, if he refuses to do so when he can - 'he shall not eat' (2 Thessalonians 3:10). This is not the only or the highest motivation (cf. Ephesians 4:28; 6:7) but it is not to be despised.

Work, and the ability to work itself, are part of God's provision. In this petition we ask God for ability and skill to obtain everyday practical necessities. 'He who works his land will have abundant food,' the Book of Proverbs says, 'but the one who chases fantasies will have his fill of poverty' (Proverbs 28:19). At the same time the Bible points out the folly of imagining that prosperity through work is simply the fruit of our own endeavours; we need God's blessing upon what we do. The rich fool who boasted to his soul, 'You have plenty of good things laid up for many years. Take life easy; eat, drink and be merry' was guilty of such folly with the disastrous result of a lost eternity (Luke 12:19ff). The things we set our hearts upon so easily lead nowhere. 'In vain you rise early and stay up late, toiling for food to eat,' the Psalmist says, 'for he grants sleep to those he loves' (Psalm 127:2). When God is left out of our reckoning, feverishness and emptiness mark human efforts to earn bread. Nowhere is this more apparent than when the Sabbath principle is ignored. God's provision does not require work on the one day in seven he gives for rest. If we break the principle, the provision we already have will easily go sour on us, as did the manna (Exodus 16:19-30).

A BLESSING TO TREASURE

A benefit of being children of our Heavenly Father is our ability to trust him for our daily needs. 'Jehovah-Jireh' - 'the Lord will provide' (Genesis 22:8,14) - should be our quiet and unpresumptuous testimony. It is not that we are simply allowed to trust him in this area of life, but we are commanded to do so. 'Therefore I tell you,' our Saviour said, 'do not worry about your life, what you will eat or drink; or about your body, what you will wear. Is not life more important than food, and the body more important than clothes?' (Matthew 6:25; Luke 12:22,23).

A great gain of being children of our Heavenly Father is the knowledge that as we give priority to the concerns expressed in the first three petitions - which we may sum up as 'his kingdom and his right-eousness' - we may be sure that our Heavenly Father will provide us with everything else we need (Matthew 6:33). 'I was young and now I am old,' the Psalmist wrote, 'yet I have never seen the righteous forsaken or their children begging bread' (Psalm 37:25). Part of our trust in God is recognising that what he chooses to give us by way of material possessions is the best for us - not least for the good of our characters and the development of our faith in his wise providence.

There is a difference between praying for material benefits - summed up in daily bread - and praying for spiritual blessings. We know that all that is in Christ is ours (1 Corinthians 3:21-23) and we are to be continually reaching after all to which God has called us in him - and not least the fruit of his Spirit in our character. Of that fruit we cannot have too much. But when it comes to physical and material benefits - the fruits of this world - we cannot be dogmatic. Our wisdom is to ask God for what he deems best.

Put another way, we should ask for physical and material benefits for spiritual ends, or, as Thomas Watson put it, 'We must aim at heaven while we are praying for earth.' Security rests not in the accu-mulation of material possessions but in God himself. 'The blessing of the LORD brings wealth, and he adds no trouble to it' (Proverbs 10:22). In the Hebrew of this verse there is a pronoun which makes it read like this, 'The blessing of the LORD **it** makes rich', that is to say, nothing else really does. Our greatest potential benefits become our greatest potential curses if the Lord is not with us; and vice versa.

The example of the Israelites in the desert, of Elijah, of missionaries, and of Christians in general, makes clear that our Father's love is not always shown by lavish provision. Our Lord Jesus Christ himself sometimes lacked bread to eat and a place to lay his head. But our Father adds what we need in the way, and at the time, he knows to be best. When we are sure that it is the Lord who adds good things to us, we may really enjoy them!

A rich gain of being children of our Heavenly Father is contentment, for this prayer teaches us to be reasonable, moderate and restrained in our desires. We are not taught to ask for wealth and abundance. There are things the world at large considers essential to life, but they are not always so (Matthew 6:32). 'Godliness with contentment is great gain' (1 Timothy 6:6). Like Paul we may learn to say, 'I know what it is to be in need, and I know what it is to have plenty. I have learned the secret of being content in any or every situation, whether well-fed or hungry, whether living in plenty or in want' (Philippians 4:12). His secret was the strength of his living Lord Jesus, communicated to him by his Spirit (Philippians 4:13).

Contentment is a vital part of Christian testimony in a greedy world. We glorify God by it. When we show ourselves satisfied with what God provides, we honour his wisdom. We testify to our assurance that all our circumstances are ordered by his good and perfect will. Like David we say, 'Lord, you have assigned me my portion and my cup; you have made my lot secure. The boundary lines have fallen for me in pleasant places; surely I have a delightful inheritance' (Psalm 16:5,6). We honour God by always rejoicing, constantly praying, and in all circumstances giving thanks (1 Thessalonians 5:16-18).

A boon of being children of our Heavenly Father is constant awareness of our dependence upon him. 'Give us today our daily bread' implies our dependence upon our Heavenly Father for food and all the benefits of this life. To recognise and to rejoice in our complete dependence upon God is a source of unsurpassed peace. The perfection of a child's relationship to its mother, for instance, is that it looks to her for everything and is never disappointed. She in turn rejoices in that relationship and is grieved and upset if her child looks to anyone else as it looks to her. We discover the full depths of our relationship to God when we not only depend upon him, but depend on him wholly, as we look to no one else.

We must not overlook the word 'daily' in the prayer: 'Give us today our **daily** bread.' There has been much discussion as to whether this means 'Give us our bread for today' or 'Give us our bread for tomorrow.' But however we interpret it, it points to everyday dependence! The debate has been resolved somewhat by the discovery of a papyrus fragment. It was actually a woman's shopping list. Against an item was this Greek word 'daily'. It was a note to remind her to buy supplies of food for the coming day. Day to day reliance upon our Heavenly Father is to characterize his children. The peace that comes from confidence in such a Father is one of the blessings of faith.

We need to avoid attitudes and life-styles which weaken our dependence upon God. The Lord Jesus underlined this when he sent his disciples out on a preaching mission: 'Take nothing for the journey, except a staff - no bread, no bag, no money in your belts' (Matthew 10:10; Mark 6:8; cf. Luke 10:4). None of these practical provisions were, or are, wrong in themselves; but the Lord Jesus was teaching his disciples conscious dependence upon God. Our own dependence upon him too needs to be honest. This is not easy to achieve in our contemporary world where we take for granted material security and many forms of government help.

A HELPFUL IF UNFASHIONABLE PRACTICE - THE GIVING OF THANKS

The invariable habit of Christians of former generations was to give thanks to God for food whenever eaten, whether in private or in public. This practice is not so prevalent or conspicuous, and yet it remains a positive way of reminding ourselves that 'our daily bread' has only one ultimate source. Our Lord Jesus set an example at the feeding of the five thousand: 'Taking the five loaves and the two fish and looking up to heaven, he gave thanks and broke the loaves' (Mark 6:41; Matthew 14:19; Luke 9:16; John 6:11), and that act of thanksgiving was remembered (John 6:23). This was his regular practice. At the Last Supper, the Lord Jesus 'took bread, gave thanks' before he broke it and gave it to the disciples and similarly with the cup (Mark 14:22,23; Matthew 26:26,27; Luke 22:17-19). In the midst of a shipwreck, Paul 'took some bread and gave thanks to God' in front of sailors and passengers (Acts 27:35)

It was the practice among the Jews for the head of the family or the host to say the blessing holding the bread in his hands. He then broke the bread, ate a piece of it himself and distributed it to those present. The Jews were instructed, 'When you have eaten and are satisfied, praise the LORD your God for the good land he has given you' (Deuteronomy 8:10). Food is to be received with thanksgiving (1 Timothy 4:3-5).

The ancient blessing for bread was: 'Blessed art thou, O Lord our God, King of the world, who bringest forth bread from the earth', and Jewish teaching was that 'It is forbidden to man to taste of this world without saying a blessing: whoever tastes of this world without saying a blessing commits unfaithfulness.'

Those who live closer to the harsh realities of life and of fending for a living may often put us to shame. British soldiers were on patrol in Sarawak, guided through the tall timbers of the deep forest by a Penan. The party stopped for their midday handout of rations and with spoons poised for action were ready to eat. Suddenly the Penan turned to them and said, 'Stop all of you. We pray before we eat!' The soldiers sheepishly lowered their cutlery to the 'as you were' position while the jungle man led them in a substantial prayer of thanks. 'Ah, you can all eat now,' he said as he opened his eyes. The Army captain who told the story remarked that all the men felt rebuked at their paganism in view of such devotion.

To give thanks unashamedly for our daily bread is part of Christian witness and testimony in a world where God is so often forgotten. Chuck Colson tells the story of sitting in a coffee shop one evening with a friend, having ordered two cheese omelettes. Then he suggested that his companion, whose name was Fred, asked the Lord's blessing on the food that would shortly be served. He writes, 'We bowed our heads. As blessings go it was a fairly long one. When we raised our heads, the waitress was standing nearby, omelettes in her hands. "Hey, were you guys praying?" She seemed surprised and spoke so loud that everyone in the small room turned to look. "Yes, we were." "Hey, that's neat. I've never seen anybody do that in here before. Are you preachers?" They explained that they were not, and told of their involvement with Prison Fellowship. As a consequence of that conversation, following upon their giving thanks before their meal, the waitress, who turned out to be a Christian who had wandered from her faith, sought God afresh.

OTHERS

'Give us today our daily bread,' is a prayer we pray not just for ourselves. We are to have others in view as we pray, and we are to keep them in mind as we receive the answers to our prayer. There is a sense in which we are not allowed to pray 'Give me today my daily bread' because God gives us bread that we may give it in turn to our brother and our neighbour.

We receive our daily bread from God in order that we may be able to help supply what others require. Paul used his tent-making not only to cater for his own needs but those of his companions, exemplifying the words of the Lord Jesus, 'It is more blessed to give than to receive' (Acts 20:34,35). We work with a deliberate view to having 'something to share with those in need' (Ephesians 4:28). To practise such principles exhibits the beauty of the Bible's teaching, as a telling story from the life of John Wesley illustrates. 'One of John Wesley's preachers named Samuel Bradburn was much esteemed as a good preacher and an excellent man. At a time when he was in straitened circumstances, Mr. Wesley sent him the following letter:

Dear Sammy,
'Trust in the Lord and do good; so shalt thou dwelt in the land and verily thou shalt be fed.'
Yours affectionately, John Wesley.
With the letter he enclosed two £5 notes.

The reply was prompt:

Rev. and Dear Sir,
I have often been struck with the beauty of the passage of Scripture quoted in your good letter, but I must confess that I never saw such useful expository notes on it before.
I am, reverend, and dear sir, your obedient and grateful servant.
S. Bradburn

God gives us everything we need - and more - so that there will not only be enough for our own wants, but plenty left to give cheerfully to others (2 Corinthians 9:7,8). If our enemy is hungry, we are to give him food to eat (Proverbs 25:21). How much more are we to be concerned for members of God's family (Galatians 6:10)! 'What good is it, my brothers, if a man claims to have faith but has no deeds? Can such faith save him?' James asks. 'Suppose a brother or sister is without clothes and daily food. If one of you says to him, "Go, I wish you well; keep warm and well fed," but does nothing about his physical needs, what good is it?' (James 2:14-16). Giving is part of our service of the saints (2 Corinthians 8:4). The Old Testament - and not least in the Book of Proverbs - established the duty and happy privilege of those in a right relationship with God to care for the poor: 'If a man shuts his ears to the cry of the poor, he too will cry out and not be answered' (Proverbs 21:13). 'A generous man will himself be blessed, for he shares his food with the poor' (Proverbs 22:9). 'The righteous care about justice for the poor' (Proverbs 29:7).
Besides the teaching of the Old Testament, the early Church had before it the example of our Lord Jesus and his disciples' giving to the needy, even though their resources must sometimes have been

slender (Luke 14:13; John 13:29). The poor should benefit from our discipleship (Matthew 19:21; Luke 18:22). From the beginning the Church felt a responsibility for the poor and underprivileged (Acts 2:44f; 4:32ff; 6:1ff). Paul was concerned for the support of others in want (Acts 20:34f), and emphasised the duty of providing for them (Romans 15:26f; 2 Corinthians 8 and 9; Galatians 2:10). Our ability to give to the poor is a worthy motive for earning money through employment (Ephesians 4:28). Those of us who are better off - 'rich in this present world' are commanded to 'do good, to be rich in good deeds, and to be generous and willing to share' (1 Timothy 6:17,18). The desperate need of the world's poor may seem beyond us, but we can all help the poor man at our gate. That was precisely where the rich man failed with regard to Lazarus, the beggar who was laid at his gate each day. No criticism is expressed of the rich man that he failed to be concerned for the world's hungry, but he did fail to help the individual whose need was daily present for his eyes to see (Luke 16:19-31).

Our bread is bread to be shared, and blessing then results for both giver and receiver. 'A generous man will himself be blessed, for he shares his food with the poor' (Proverbs 22:9). As we give, God so often performs the miracle of supplying and multiplying our resources so that we can give again (2 Corinthians 9:10). It was said of a Christian man in the area in which David Livingstone, the missionary, was born, 'Dale gives his money away, but God shovels it back again.' Christian giving is one of the paradoxes of the Christian life: 'Give, and it will be given to you. A good measure, pressed down, shaken together and running over, will be poured into your lap. For with the measure you use, it will be measured to you' (Luke 6:38).

We pray 'Give us today our daily bread' so that, among other things, we may have bread - and all that it represents - to share with our missionary representatives, our pastors, the needy within our church fellowships, and the poor and underprivileged of the world. There are specific individuals for whom our Father wants us to provide bread as he provides it for us.

UNASHAMED DEPENDANTS

Unashamed dependants is the fifth picture the Lord's Prayer gives of what it means to be a Christian. As unashamed dependants, we pray, 'Give us today our daily bread.' All the good we have, we owe to God. We want to seek first his kingdom, and hand over all other concerns to him. While in our contemporary society we tend to be sheltered from urgent material need, we do not want to lose for a moment our awareness of dependence upon God.

Chapter 6

Forgiven debtors

'Forgive us our debts as we also have forgiven our debtors'

If daily bread represents our basic material or physical wants, forgiveness sums up our first spiritual need. That this petition comes immediately after the prayer for daily bread is a reminder that material benefits are of little use, and provide limited happiness, if we do not possess spiritual blessings and especially the forgiveness of our sins. Forgiveness follows daily bread, and in the Greek New Testament the two petitions are significantly linked together by the word 'and'. Daily bread - and all it represents - cannot be enjoyed if we do not live in harmony with others.

Those of us who live in the more affluent parts of the world have to admit that our comparative wealth does not guarantee benefits such as peace of mind, harmonious human relationships, and stable family life; in fact, it almost seems that the opposite is the case. We are not simply physical beings with only physical and material needs; but rather creatures made originally in God's image with a vital spiritual dimension to our life. Lived without a right relationship to God, life lacks its most essential constituent for true happiness. We need daily forgiveness as much as daily bread. Our daily bread tastes better when we know God's forgiveness. God is not only the Giver, he is also the Forgiver.

While other petitions of the Lord's Prayer can be found in some form or other in Jewish prayers contemporary with Jesus' ministry, this petition is not to be found. The forgiveness the gospel proclaims is new.

A MAIN THEME OF THE GOSPEL

Forgiveness is a main theme of the gospel. John the Baptist was our

Lord Jesus Christ's forerunner. Forgiveness was prominent in his message: 'John came ... preaching a baptism of repentance for the forgiveness of sins' (Mark 1:4; Luke 3:3; cf. Luke 1:76,77). Our Lord Jesus came both preaching and **giving** forgiveness. His first miracle recorded in Matthew, Mark and Luke draws attention to the priority of forgiveness over physical healing (Matthew 9:1-8; Mark 2:1-12; Luke 5:17-26). Looking at the paralysed man, lowered dramatically through the roof of the house to Jesus, the reaction of the crowds was then - as it would be now - 'This man needs to be healed of his paralysis.' But Jesus' first words were, 'Take heart, son; your sins are forgiven' (Matthew 9:2). One day the man's body would die and his physical suffering would be over. But at his death, the vital question would be the well-being of his never-dying soul. That, therefore, was his major need; and Jesus dealt with that first. Forgiveness is an essential part of the offer of the gospel (Acts 2:38); to reject the gospel is to forfeit all possibility of forgiveness (John 20:23).

TOP OF THE LIST

When David urged his soul not to forget all God's benefits, first in his list was the forgiveness of his sins (Psalm 103:3). Important as physical healing, ransom from death, and personal experience of God's love and compassion were, nothing in David's experience so expressed the wonder of God's grace as his forgiveness of David's sins.

Forgiveness of sins likewise comes top of any list of God's benefits through his Son Jesus Christ. The wonder of fellowship with God the Father and with his Son, the indwelling of his Spirit, and the assurance of heaven become our personal experience only as we know God's forgiveness through his overflowing kindness in our Lord Jesus (Ephesians 1:7). Peter was expressly sent by God to proclaim the good news of the gospel to Cornelius, a Gentile, and he summed up its message about the Lord Jesus Christ by declaring: 'All the prophets testify about him that everyone who believes in him receives forgiveness of sins through his name' (Acts 10:43). As Isaiah promised, the Lord Jesus is God's righteous servant who justifies many by bearing their iniquities (Isaiah 53:11). He is the One who has made possible what God promised through Jeremiah: 'I will forgive their wickedness and will remember their sins no more' (Jeremiah 31:34). Through the merits of his atoning sacrifice, the 'fountain ... to cleanse ... from sin and impurity' that Zechariah promised (13:1) has been opened. The Lord Jesus is 'the sun of righteousness' Malachi anticipated, risen 'with healing in its wings' (4:2).

DEBTS AND TRESPASSES

According to the part of the world in which we live, and the church background to which we belong, we say either 'debts' or 'trespasses'. A debt is a sum owed, but in later Judaism it became a common term for sin. 'Debts' arises directly from Matthew's gospel (Matthew 6:12) and 'trespasses' indirectly from Luke, who uses the usual New Testament word for 'sins' (Luke 11:4). The verb from which sin comes originally - **hamartia** - meant to miss the mark, to lose so as not to share in something. Sin is both a falling away from a relationship of faithfulness to God and also disobedience to his commands, his law. The use of the word 'trespasses' seems to spring from the Book of Common Prayer. We need have no argument with its use in that sin is transgression, that is to say, the violation of God's law (1 John 3:4). When we do what God's law forbids, we transgress or trespass (Daniel 9:11).

Sin - or trespass - conveys the thought of our falling short of what God demands; debt also implies the ingratitude to God which is behind our sins, and our obligation to answer to him for them. By our sins we have wronged God, and we cannot ourselves right or repay the wrong. Sadly, it is a debt that we daily increase and multiply.

GOD'S PREROGATIVE

The authority to forgive sins belongs to God alone. If we think of sins as unpayable debts, only the creditor can cancel our debt. Overwhelmed by his sinfulness before God, Isaiah cried, 'Woe to me! I am ruined! For I am a man of unclean lips, and I live among a people of unclean lips, and my eyes have seen the King, the Lord Almighty' (Isaiah 6:5). It required God to take the initiative to send him cleansing by the removal of his guilt and the atoning of his sin as a live coal from the altar was placed upon his mouth (Isaiah 6:6,7).

The crowds who witnessed Jesus pronouncing forgiveness were right to exclaim, 'Who can forgive sins but God alone?' (Mark 2:7; Luke 5:21). Centuries before David said to God, 'With you there is forgiveness; therefore you are feared' (Psalm 130:4), and Micah asked, 'Who is a God like you, who pardons sin and forgives the transgression of the remnant of his inheritance? You do not stay angry for ever but delight to show mercy' (Micah 7:18).

GOD'S PREROGATIVE AS JUDGE

Forgiveness - our release from the penalty of our sins - is an act of God as the divine Judge. The glorious truth of the gospel is that God the righteous Judge has provided a propitiatory sacrifice for our sins which fully squares with his justice, so that our guilt and liability to his wrath may be removed, and he may declare us 'Not guilty!'

Propitiation is not a word we use in everyday speech, but it is one for which there is really no adequate replacement, much as modern translations of the Bible try. The sad background to the word are the sobering truths that we deserve God's wrath on account of our sin, and that his justice rightly demands that our sin should be punished. The death of the Lord Jesus perfectly satisfied God's holy judgment upon us as sinners so that his wrath is removed from us: this is what is meant when the Bible declares that the Lord Jesus is the propitiation for our sins (1 John 2:2).

Forgiveness and justification go together. We catch a glimpse of this in the story Jesus told of the two men who went up to the Temple to pray, one a Pharisee and the other a tax collector. 'The tax collector ... beat his breast and said, "God, have mercy on me, a sinner"' (Luke 18:13). Literally, he cried, 'God be propitious to me, the sinner.' Convicted of his sin, he was aware he required a propitiation. He went home, we are told, not only forgiven, but 'justified before God' (Luke

18:14). As well as being pardoned, he was declared 'Not guilty' because of the propitiation God provided.

God's forgiveness completely accords with his justice. That is why God can say, 'Come now, let us **reason** together ... Though your sins are like scarlet, they shall be as white as snow; though they are red as crimson, they shall be like wool' (Isaiah 1:18). It is reasonable for God to forgive sins on account of what he, the righteous Judge, has done about them. God can forgive our sins and still remain faithful and just!

COSTLY TO GOD

Forgiveness is nearly always more of a problem to the forgiver than the forgiven. Forgiveness is no easy thing for God. While he is loving, he is also just, righteous and holy. He is as much light as he is love. As the word 'propitiation' shows, God supremely demonstrated his love by giving his Son to be the One who satisfies his justice, righteousness and holiness by his death in our place. God's holy anger against our sins - which both his justice and law rightly demand - fell upon his Son in place of us. No wonder our Saviour cried, 'My God, my God, why have you forsaken me?'(Mark 15:34) He was actually forsaken as he accepted the penalty and punishment of our sins.

Forgiveness is possible only through the shedding of blood. This was taught in symbol in the Old Testament, and finds its fulfilment in the New Covenant in Jesus' blood. It is his blood which removes all our guilt, and his obedience which covers us with merit. Taking the cup at the Last Supper, our Lord said, 'This is my blood of the new covenant, which is poured out for many for the forgiveness of sins' (Matthew 26:28). God raised his Son from the dead to give us the assurance of forgiveness (Acts 5:31; 1 Corinthians 15:17). Every experience of God's forgiveness is on account of his grace to us in Jesus Christ.

GLORIOUS PICTURES

To ensure that we appreciate and rest in his perfect forgiveness, God provides pictures and illustrations throughout the Bible. He puts our sins as far as the east is from the west (Psalm 103:12). Here the picture is of distance: we cannot measure how far God puts our sins from us. He sweeps away our sins like a cloud, like the morning mist (Isaiah 44:22). Here the picture is of removal and obliteration. He treads our sins underfoot and hurls them into the depths of the sea (Micah 7:19). Here the picture is of his breaking the power of our sins and hiding them, where no-one can find them. He wipes out our sins (Acts 3:19). Here the picture is of erasure or washing. God clears our slate, and no trace can be found of our sins, even in his perfect records. A contemporary illustration is the pressing of the cancel button on a calculator, so that every record is removed from its memory. God cancels our debt (Colossians 2:14). As Paul puts it, God forgives us 'according to the riches of his grace' (Ephesians 1:7).

Forgiveness is not some abstract theological concept: it is our Lord Jesus Christ coming to us in the name of the Father, and saying, 'Do not be afraid. Your sins are forgiven. God is at peace with you. Be glad!' Imagine our sins placed in a huge container, loaded on to a ship, and transported to the deepest ocean. Then see them cast overboard into the sea. Watch them sink to the bottom, out of sight. Look at the sea now, calm and peaceful, with the sun shining on it - the sunshine of our Heavenly Father's love.

All such pictures are different ways of saying the same thing: when God forgives, he forgets. God looks upon pardoned sinners as if they had never sinned: 'I will forgive their wickedness and will remember their sins no more' (Jeremiah 31:34). Though we may remember them, God does not. Though Satan, the enemy of our souls, raises the matter; God never does. Even as the father of the prodigal son made no mention of his son's tragic disobedience, and its consequences, neither does our Father. Rather, he receives us with joy.

AS URGENT AS DAILY BREAD

Daily forgiveness is necessary as often and regularly as our daily bread. This petition in the Lord's Prayer is a great encouragement because it shows that we may pray for forgiveness as often as we require it.

Once received, forgiveness needs to be constantly renewed. Jesus taught this when he washed the disciples' feet. In the week before his death, when the disciples were sharing a meal together, the Lord Jesus 'got up from the meal, took off his outer clothing, and wrapped a towel round his waist. After that, he poured water into a basin and began to wash his disciples' feet, drying them with the towel that was wrapped round him' (John 13:4,5). Peter's impetuous response was, 'No, you shall never wash my feet.' 'Unless I wash you, you have no part with me,' Jesus replied. 'Then, Lord,' Peter replied, 'not just my feet but my hands and my head as well!' Jesus explained, 'A person who has had a bath needs only to wash his feet; his whole body is clean' (John 13:8-10). Conversion and new birth are like a bath: all our sins are forgiven and pardoned. We are made clean, and we enter into fellowship with God.

But sin is not eradicated from our lives when we are born into God's family. While we hate sin as never before, and its power is broken, nevertheless day by day we still sin and fall short of being the people we ought to be. Sinning, we do not lose our salvation, but we forfeit our experience of fellowship with God. All the time unforgiven sin is in our life we fail to know the happiness God intends through forgiveness and cleansing (Psalm 32:1,2). Undeclared sin is unforgiven sin (Psalm 32:3). We need daily cleansing, and this was the lesson Jesus taught.

No doubt Peter had had a thorough wash or bath at the beginning of the day. But as he walked through the dusty streets of Jerusalem to the upper room, his feet had become dirty. He did not require another bath but he did need his feet to be washed. So it is that as we live in a sinful world with its temptations to our fallen senses and desires, we get 'our feet dirty', spoiling our fellowship with God, and we need afresh God's forgiveness. As we confess our sins, he can be depended upon to forgive us and to cleanse us from every wrong (1 John 1:9). Our fellowship with him is then immediately restored. The merits of our Saviour's blood guarantee our restoration to fellowship with God every time we confess our sins.

We do well to keep short accounts with God. To delay to seek his forgiveness, perhaps until the end of the day, may mean we spoil most of the day. But confessing our sins, the moment the Holy Spirit makes us aware of them, the remainder of the day may be lived for God with a clear conscience. The restoration of our relationship to God through his forgiveness renews our gratitude to him - an indebtedness that leads to holy living.

AN OBLIGATION

As much stress should be placed on the second part of this petition in the Lord's Prayer as on the first. According to Matthew's gospel, we are taught not only to ask, 'Forgive us our debts' but to go on to say, '**as** we forgive our debtors,' literally 'in proportion to'. Luke quotes another occasion when our Lord said, '**for** we forgive' instead of '**as** we forgive' (Luke 11:4). Literally Luke writes, 'for indeed (we) ourselves forgive everyone owing to us' - in other words, it is in the present tense. We are to show a continual readiness to forgive.

God's forgiveness places an obligation upon us to forgive others. Living as some of our brothers and sisters in Christ do in brutal and war-torn environments where awful atrocities take place, this is no easy duty. We do not naturally possess the ability to forgive. Our natural human reaction to any wrong done to us is summed up in an inscription found on the monument to Sulla, a prominent statesman, in Rome: 'No friend ever did me so much good, or enemy so much harm, but I repaid him with interest.' But as Christians we do not forgive because it is easy, but because it is commanded.

The petition teaches that forgiveness of others is possible as we ourselves are forgiven by God. A history of the Wycliffe Bible Translators describes the conversion of an Indian mayor of a Mexican town. 'It was not long until he put away the pistol which he carried to shoot his political enemies who had made an attempt on his life. He purchased three New Testaments and sent them to his main enemies with a letter to each. He explained in the letters that through this Book he had learned to forgive them, and he wanted them to read it too so that they could forgive him, and thus they could become good friends.' Forgiveness is the proper Christian alternative to judging others (Luke 6:37).

On Monday, 8th November, 1993, an obituary appeared in the *Daily Telegraph* of Alfred Bosshardt, a British born missionary of the China Inland Mission (OMF) who had died, aged 96. He was one of those handful of foreigners, mainly foreign missionary captives, who had been forced to struggle 2,500 miles across China on foot as a prisoner on the legendary 'Long March' of the Communists in the mid-1930s. He was arraigned as an 'imperialist spy' before a howling Communist mob in a town square. He was repeatedly sentenced to death in support of ransom demands. He was stripped and beaten with bamboo rods. The obituary notice mentioned two things which struck me. First, throughout his ordeal Bosshardt managed to show compassion to his captors. 'Using a sword, he fashioned a crochet hook from a chopstick so that he could make woollen caps and gloves for his guards.' Secondly, 'in the horror of the Long March he put aside all thoughts of hatred and told himself: "God loves these people, so I must love them too". This fundamental essence of Christian teaching clearly informed the whole of his remarkable life.'

A CONDITION

More than a duty, forgiving others is a condition of our own experience of God's forgiveness. We are not to expect mercy from him if we are unwilling to show it to others. As we have indicated earlier, our forgiving others is not to be thought of as a good work that merits God's forgiveness; but it is to be thought of as the removal of an obstacle to our experiencing God's forgiveness. Our forgiveness of others is not a cause of God forgiving us; but it is a condition. Even something which is a complete gift often requires action on our part. Imagine a friend sends us a complimentary ticket for a concert or a sporting event. The initiative is entirely our friend's, and there is nothing we have to do to merit it. Nevertheless, to enjoy the event, we must present the ticket. God's act of forgiving us is dependent entirely on his grace, and not at all upon our works, even our forgiving others. But we are in a position to ask for forgiveness from God only if we are willing to forgive others.

Jesus related a telling story to illustrate this condition of God's forgiveness. 'The kingdom of heaven,' he said, 'is like a king who wanted to settle accounts with his servants. As he began the settlement, a man who owed him ten thousand talents was brought to him. Since he was not able to pay, the master ordered that he and his wife and his children and all that he had be sold to repay the debt. The servant fell on his knees before him. "Be patient with me," he begged, "and I will pay back everything." The servant's master took pity on him, cancelled the debt and let him go. But when that servant went out, he found one of his fellow-servants who owed him a hundred denarii. He grabbed him and began to choke him. "Pay back what you owe me!" he demanded. His fellow-servant fell to his knees and begged him, "Be patient with me, and I will pay you back." But he refused. Instead, he went off and had the man thrown into prison until he could pay the debt. When the other servants saw what had happened, they were greatly distressed and went and told their master everything that had happened. Then the master called the servant in. "You wicked servant," he said, "I cancelled all that debt of yours because you begged me to. Shouldn't you have had mercy on your fellow-servant just as I had on you?" In anger his master turned him over to the jailers to be tortured, until he should pay back all he owed' (Matthew 18:23-34). The two sums involved represented the difference between £5,000,000 and £10!

Jesus followed this story at once with the statement: 'This is how my heavenly Father will treat each of you unless you forgive your brother from your heart' (Matthew 18:35). We dare not minimize the seriousness of this. The only petition in the Lord's Prayer which our Lord chose to amplify was this one concerning forgiveness: 'For if you forgive men when they sin against you, your heavenly Father will also forgive you. But if you do not forgive men their sins, your Father will not forgive your sins' (Matthew 6:14,15). Sadly, experience shows that we do not always take this truth to heart.

One of the major hindrances of blessing in our churches, in our families and our personal relationships is the absence of the practice of forgiveness; and the consequent forfeiture of the constant renewal of God's forgiveness and conscious fellowship with him. If we neglect the exercise of forgiveness, we will soon lose our enjoyment of God's pardon. A general principle the Lord Jesus taught applies particularly here because it was in this context that it was established: 'Give, and it will be given to you' (Luke 6:38). If we pray the Lord's Prayer with hatred and resentment in our hearts, we pray for our own condemnation. 'Get rid of all bitterness, rage and anger, brawling and slander, along with every kind of malice,' Paul urged. All such attitudes grieve the Holy Spirit (Ephesians 4:30,31). Rather we are exhorted, 'Be kind and compassionate to one another, forgiving each other, just as in Christ God forgave you' (Ephesians 4:32). Paul was simply amplifying Jesus' words: 'Therefore, if you are offering your gift at the altar and there remember that your brother has something against you, leave your gift there in front of the altar. First go and be reconciled to your brother; then come and offer your gift' (Matthew 5:23,24). (When the Lord Jesus spoke these words the Temple in Jerusalem was standing, and the altar was situated in front of the Temple, and was where sacrifices were offered.)

Forgiving others is a prerequisite of our own daily experience of God's forgiveness. The way in which we forgive is the way in which we will be forgiven (Luke 6:37). This petition is calculated to cure the hypocrisy of not dealing with others as God deals with us. Unforgiving, we live uninfluenced by the gift of God's salvation we have received. There is to be an exact correspondence between our own experience of God's forgiveness and how we forgive one another (Ephesians 4:32). Forgiveness is an essential part of the new 'clothes' Christians are to wear. It is one of the many evidences that we are really God's children, for his children increasingly bear his likeness.

THE ROOT OF MANY PROBLEMS

A superintendent of a mental hospital has said he would be able to send a large percentage of his patients home cured if only they could be assured of forgiveness. How different and better much of church history would have been if forgiveness had been practised! What a difference it would make to our churches if forgiveness always prevailed. It is the essential oil for human relationships without which they not only grind to a halt, but go terribly wrong.

Asking for forgiveness is as important as giving it. Sometimes parents need to apologise to sons and daughters, and husbands and wives to their partner. One night a father sat down and wrote a letter to his daughter, a daughter who acknowledged that she had inherited the same inflammable and unreasonable temper. 'I'm so sorry that I upset you ... Please accept my apology ... Your always loving (but too often rude and irritable) Daddy.' Years later, after her father's death, the daughter remembered that letter with gratitude, and the example it provided.

Returning to the USA after being a prisoner of war in Vietnam, Howard Rutledge, an American pilot, converted while a captive, longed that when he got home he might put into practice what one of his Christian fellow prisoners had taught him: '"Let not the sun go down on your wrath" (Ephesians 4:26).' His friend had explained that 'he and his wife Margaret had determined in their marriage never to go to bed before an argument had been settled, the apology made, the angry words forgiven.' That brief passage from Ephesians 4 really made sense to this new Christian, for often, he wrote, 'I had lain awake at night too proud to say, "I'm sorry," and both of us could feel the hurt.'

A wife related to me a vivid memory of an incident in her relationship with her husband. She and her husband had a guest house and usually had about six students or missionaries living with them. One Sunday morning as they were having breakfast before her husband left for North London to preach in a church, one of the girls at the table made a cheeky remark to her husband, and he answered in the same vein. His wife rebuked him, and he replied to her in an unkind manner, leaving the table, and went out of the room closing the door none too gently, and set off on his journey in the car. His wife was far from happy at such a departure but could not do anything until the evening. She felt she had been too hasty and wanted to say she was sorry. Just before she herself was leaving for church, she had a phone call from her husband. 'In a few minutes I'll be at the church, and will be getting ready to preach; but I cannot do this until I ask your forgiveness.' When he returned home that evening, they rejoiced together and the husband testified, 'I have preached for many years, but never with such power as I experienced today.' The wife's comment to me was, 'How gracious is our God! We were together for forty years and our mutual trust in the Lord and each other grew as the years passed.'

Forgiveness so often cements human relationships. Charles Reid, the biographer of the late Sir Malcolm Sargent, the conductor, records how Sir Malcolm had an argument while rehearsing Beethoven's *Eroica* symphony. He asked the second horn to do something Beethoven did not require. The principal horn, James Brown, stood up and spoke up for his colleague. Sir Malcolm walked off the stage, leaving the orchestra in a hubbub. The sympathy of the orchestra was with the conductor rather than with the hornists. But Sir Malcolm thought better of his action. He asked James Brown to come and see him. James Brown decided to take the entire horn section - five players - with him. They expected, I think, a confrontation. Sir Malcolm 'greeted his visitors with a smile of relief and said: "Gentlemen, I never hold a grudge against any person. On this occasion I was very wrong. Can we shake on it?" He went down the line, gripping each player by the hand. Taking Brown aside later ... he had won a loyal friend.'

COSTLY TO US

Forgiveness is always costly. It may mean forgiving the same person seven times in a day (Luke 17:3,4); but it is still right to do so for that is what our Saviour taught.

Pioneer missionary to Africa David Livingstone and his family suffered much through malicious gossip and idle talk. Twenty years afterwards the hurt was still there. Writing to a friend, he said, 'I often think I have forgiven, as I hope to be forgiven, but the remembrance of the slander often comes boiling up, although I hate to think of it. You must remember me in your prayers that more of the spirit of Christ may be imparted to me.' It was no easy thing for Livingstone to forgive, but with the help of the Spirit of Christ he did! In the Tupuri language of the Cameroons and Chad, to 'forgive' is to 'blow our insides out'. If dust settles on anything, they blow it off. In the same way, the heart is to be cleared of anything which spoils life. Translating Ephesians 4:32 back from Tupuri becomes, 'Blow your insides out for one another. God blows insides out for you with Jesus.'

NOT OVERLOOKING THE OBVIOUS

Forgiveness is not ours until we seek it with repentance. It is easy to overlook this simple truth so clearly taught by this petition's inclusion in the Lord's Prayer. When we first experienced God's forgiveness, we repented of our sin and called upon the name of the Lord. There was nothing haphazard or casual about it; it was earnest and deliberate. Similarly as we progress in the Christian life, our sins after conversion are not forgiven until we repent of them. Although we no longer have cause to fear God's wrath and judgment upon them, we may as his children provoke his displeasure.

The whole of the Christian life is to be one of continual repentance, that is to say, a daily turning from sin to God, and a daily asking for his forgiveness where we have not turned away from sin quickly enough. Repentance rightly becomes a principle and a habit, and we see our wrongdoing no longer as attractive but as loathsome. Our repentance - like our forgiveness of others - does not merit our pardon by God, but it prepares the way for it. As soon as we repent, our feet are effectively on the path of returning to the Lord.

David Yang Shaotang worked in China with a number of missionaries belonging to the China Inland Mission (now the OMF), one of whom was David Adeney. Going to David Yang's room one day, David Adeney found him 'stretched out upon the mud floor of his simple room, crying out to God, confessing his own weakness and sinfulness and asking for cleansing and the filling of the Holy Spirit. As Pastor Yang was already a man whose life was characterized by humility and Christlikeness, David was amazed to see him humbling himself before God in this way. It made an indelible impression on him.' David Adeney said, 'I realized that however greatly a man might be used in the service of the Lord Jesus, he is nevertheless constantly in need of repentance and of waiting upon God.'

A PLACE FOR SELF-EXAMINATION

If we are to pray daily for a renewal of God's forgiveness - something this petition implies - to do so with integrity there must be a willingness to examine ourselves. We sometimes take fright at engaging in self-examination because of the danger of introspection; and certainly some are more prone to that peril than others. The safest, and therefore best, means of self-examination is to test ourselves daily by the Scriptures that we read. If we read the Bible systematically we expose ourselves to all of God's revealed will. (Not to read the Bible systematically leads to a deficient knowledge of God's truth and spiritual weakness.) Testing our lives by what we read each day is the safest spiritual health check, especially as we strive to align our life to what we daily discover God requires. A paradox is that the more we try to be obedient, the more aware we become of our sin and failure - and, therefore, of our need of God's forgiveness. But a mark of godly men and women is conscious and daily dependence upon his grace.

A UNIQUE SECRET OF HAPPINESS

The Book of Psalms expresses often the joy of God's forgiveness: 'Blessed is he whose transgressions are forgiven, whose sins are covered. Blessed is the man whose sin the Lord does not count against him and in whose spirit is no deceit ... Rejoice in the LORD and be glad, you righteous; sing, all you who are upright in heart' (Psalm 32:1,2,11). The upright are those to whom God not only grants forgiveness but credits righteousness - not through their own works - but through the sacrifice of Jesus Christ on their behalf (Romans 4:6-8). Our Lord Jesus is our only refuge as we review the past. We do not deal with our past by running away from it. It needs to be faced up to, acknowledged and dealt with.

Forgiveness is the only way of dealing with the past - and with our personal past. We cannot relive it; and we can seldom remedy it. But God can deal with it! When we are right with God, and reflect his forgiveness in our own forgiveness of others, we hear our Saviour's whisper that all is forgiven, irrespective of how sad and shameful our past.

To forgive others provides a unique happiness, no matter how badly they may have harmed us. Instead of hurt, there is healing. When Joseph forgave his brothers their sins against him, not only were they happy, but he was - in the deepest sense. Luther said, 'My soul is too glad and too great to be at heart the enemy of any man.'

A WONDER THAT INCREASES

When we ultimately see God in his holiness and understand perfectly the destruction from which we have been saved, we shall marvel all the more at the magnificence and perfection of his forgiveness. It is no wonder that the saints in heaven - believers who have already died - are described as praising the Lamb who was slain. Centuries ago, Thomas Watson put it well, 'A man that goes over a narrow bridge in the night, and next morning sees the danger he was in, how miraculously he escaped, is filled with admiration; so when God shows a man how near he was falling into hell, how that gulf is passed, and all his sins are pardoned, is amazed, and cries out, "Who is a God like thee, that pardoneth iniquity?"'

A SPRING OF GRATITUDE

The Christian experience of God's forgiveness pinpoints the foremost spring of gratitude - a spring which never stops bursting forth. We overflow with thanksgiving (Colossians 2:7). While the Christian life brings undeniable duties, lived properly it is essentially a life of thankful indebtedness to God. When we live in fellowship with God - a fellowship which demands that we constantly confess our sins as they occur and receive afresh his pardon - we appreciate that we owe more to his grace in the Lord Jesus than we can ever express.

Luke records how 'one of the Pharisees invited Jesus to have dinner with him, so he went to the Pharisee's house and reclined at the table. When a woman who had lived a sinful life in that town learned that

Jesus was eating at the Pharisee's house, she brought an alabaster jar of perfume, and as she stood behind him at his feet weeping, she began to wet his feet with her tears. Then she wiped them with her hair, kissed them and poured perfume on them. When the Pharisee who had invited him saw this, he said to himself, "If this man were a prophet, he would know who is touching him and what kind of woman she is - that she is a sinner." Jesus answered him, "Simon, I have something to tell you." "Tell me, teacher," he said. "Two men owed money to a certain money-lender. One owed him five hundred denarii, and the other fifty. Neither of them had the money to pay him back, so he cancelled the debts of both. Now which of them will love him more?" Simon replied, "I suppose the one who had the bigger debt cancelled." "You have judged correctly," Jesus said. Then he turned towards the woman and said to Simon, "Do you see this woman? I came into your house. You did not give me any water for my feet, but she wet my feet with her tears and wiped them with her hair. You did not give me a kiss, but this woman, from the time I entered, has not stopped kissing my feet. You did not put oil on my head, but she has poured perfume on my feet. Therefore, I tell you, her many sins have been forgiven - for she loved much. But he who has been forgiven little loves little." Then Jesus said to her, "Your sins are forgiven"' (Luke 7:36-48).

The original meaning of the word 'grace' was that which prompts or promotes joy. God's grace certainly does that, and we can understand why Christians took the word over and made it even more meaningful. It is the grace of God's forgiveness that stirs up within us a desire to obey God, and to live for him: 'I run in the path of your commands, for you have set my heart free' (Psalm 119:32). We do not strive to keep God's Law in order to become his sons and daughters, but having become such we now obey out of gratitude. Similarly, it is our experience of his grace that teaches us to be generous to others, even opening up our wallets and purses in a way we once would not have thought possible.

We cannot sum up Christian doctrine better than by one word - grace; and similarly we may summarize Christian ethics as gratitude. It cannot be without significance that the identical Greek word is used for both - grace when speaking of God, and gratitude when referring to us.

'Christ's love compels us ... He died ... that those who live should no longer live for themselves but for him who died for them and was raised again' (2 Corinthians 5:14,15).

Gratitude is one of the best human emotions, and it is a distinctive mark of the Christian. It may be regarded as the sum of a Christian's duty: when God has our gratitude, he has everything else. 'It is probable that in most of us the spiritual life is impoverished and stunted because we give so little place to gratitude. It is more important to thank God for blessings received than to pray for them beforehand' (William Temple). Paul's devoted service sprang out of his deep experience of God's forgiveness in the Lord Jesus and his abundant grace (1 Timothy 1:12-16). Gratitude is like oil to the machinery of our obedience to our Saviour; it makes us move faster.

A PRAYER CONSISTENT WITH OTHER REQUESTS

As children of God, able to call him 'Our Father', we are duty-bound and privileged to reflect his forgiving nature. His Name is hallowed, his kingdom advanced, and his will done as we exercise forgiveness after the perfect pattern of his.

FORGIVEN DEBTORS

Forgiven debtors is the sixth picture the Lord's Prayer provides of what it means to be a Christian. Forgiven much, we love much. Forgiven much, we forgive, no matter how costly, since we will never have to forgive others as much as God has had to forgive us. Our forgiveness of others will never be as costly as ours was for God to achieve.

Chapter 7

Guided travellers and grateful ex-prisoners

'Lead us not into temptation but deliver us from
the evil one'

The petitions of the Lord's Prayer are interlocked; they fit and
hang together. The daily nature of our battle against sin is high-
lighted by this request following on immediately from the appeal
for forgiveness, and its being linked with it by the word 'and'. Our experience of forgiveness does not lessen our concern about our sin; rather it
heightens our sensitivity to it, and our desire to avoid it. Forgiven much,
our repentance deepens, along with an increasing hatred of the sins that
so easily entangle us.

To begin with, the first half of this petition appears the more difficult
because of two questions we are compelled to ask. First, is it temptations or trials which are in view here, since the Greek word translated
'temptation' can mean either according to the context? Secondly, if
temptations are included, does God ever lead us into temptation?
Fortunately other parts of the Bible provide the answers, and so does
the Lord's Prayer itself.

NOT AN EASY DISTINCTION

In theory it is easy enough to distinguish trials from temptations, and
vice versa. Temptations always have to do with something evil or
wrong: either they come unmistakeably from the evil one or they
involve doing something that is plainly bad.

Testings, however, are not necessarily evil at all. Our faith may be tested, by God withholding something from us, or by difficulties through which we have to pass.

But in practice a thin line often separates trials from temptations. What God allows or sends as a testing of our faith, Satan will all too often try to turn into a temptation. As Thomas Brooks (1608-1680) wrote, 'Times of affliction often prove times of great temptations, and therefore afflictions are called temptations.' The enemy of souls may endeavour to use a testing to tempt us to doubt God: that is precisely what he did in the Garden of Eden to our first parents. The proper test of Adam's and Eve's obedience which God imposed by the forbidden nature of the tree of the knowledge of good and evil, Satan - in the guise of the serpent - used as a means of tempting them to doubt God's motives in the prohibition. 'You will not surely die,' the serpent said. 'For God knows that when you eat of it your eyes will be opened, and you will be like God, knowing good and evil' (Genesis 3:4,5). When we are tested, we may be at a low physical ebb, and Satan will invariably aim temptations at our weakest point.

A CRUCIAL CONSEQUENCE OF THE FALL

Basic truths are always in danger of being taken for granted, and one such is the Fall (Genesis 3). There can be no realistic overcoming of sin, and of temptation to sin, if we do not face up to, and take into our thinking, the fallen nature we possess. We are not told why God allowed the Fall, and there is a mystery about it which we are not able to explore. What the Bible does teach is that when Adam sinned, we also sinned. God imputed to us Adam's guilt, just - as in his grace - he imputes to believers the Lord Jesus Christ's righteousness. We were born fallen men and women: we were sinful before we sinned.

The Bible expresses our sinfulness as a consequence of the Fall in a variety of ways, and the most simple and yet profound is its analysis of our hearts. In the Bible the heart describes the centre of our inner life, taking in our feelings, longings, decisions, responses and even our conscience. It is the fountain from which all our actions proceed (Luke 6:45). Our Lord Jesus explains, 'What comes out of a man is what makes him "unclean". For from within, out of men's hearts, come evil thoughts, sexual immorality, theft, murder, adultery, greed, malice, deceit, lewdness, envy, slander, arrogance and folly. All these evils come from inside and make a man "unclean"' (Mark 7:20-23). The heart is 'the wellspring of life' (Proverbs 4:23): it is 'deceitful above all things and beyond cure' (Jeremiah 17:9). Our contemporary world wonders why it is that we can master technology but not human behaviour; and only the Bible gives a satisfactory explanation for that.

What changes our hearts for the better is a right relationship to God through our Lord Jesus Christ: good then begins to be stored up in our hearts as we live in glad obedience to him (Luke 6:43-49). But never in this life do we lose our evil heart and its tendencies. Left to ourselves, we quickly revert to our heart's evil practices. If we stop living a life of obedience, we find bad tendencies gaining the upper hand in our heart and then life.

Our temptations are not simply Satan's fault - to put all the blame on him is all too easy. Rather the fault is equally with the pull of our sinful desires which find sin attractive (James 1:14). While it is wonderfully true that God's Law is now written on our heart as believers and the law of the Spirit of life sets us free from the law of sin and death, it is also true that if we do not walk in obedience to God's Law and the Holy Spirit we soon find that other law at work in us - that law that leads to sin and spoils our fellowship with God (Romans 7:21-23).

A RELEVANT INTERPRETATION

One particular interpretation of this petition would almost certainly have first come to mind to a Jewish audience in a way it may not immediately occur to us. Psalm 95:7-11 recalls how the Israelites 'tempted' or put God to the test. Travelling from place to place as God had directed, the Israelites 'camped at Rephidim, but there was no water for the people to drink. So they quarrelled with Moses and said, "Give us water to drink."' Moses had insight to realise that they were questioning God's providence, and doubting his love. 'They tested the LORD saying, "Is the LORD among us or not?"' (Exodus 17:1,2,7). Verses 7,

8 and 9 of Psalm 95 read, 'Today, if you hear his voice, do not harden your hearts as you did at Meribah, as you did that day at Massah in the desert, where your fathers tested and tried me, though they had seen what I did.'

The place where the Israelites doubted God was called **Massah** (which means **testing**), not because it was where Israel was tested, but where Israel tested God. God had done great things for them; but instead of trusting him, they clamoured for a new 'sign' to prove that he was among them. God's condemnation followed; and Psalm 95:10,11 records God's response: 'For forty years I was angry with that generation; I said, "They are a people whose hearts go astray, and they have not known my ways." So I declared on oath in my anger, "They shall never enter my rest."' The writer to the Hebrews comments, 'So we see that they were not able to enter, because of their unbelief' (Hebrews 3:19).

'Lead us not into temptation' has as one of its applications for us, therefore, the prayer, 'Lord, save us from those situations where doubting your Word, we refuse to take you at your Word, and we seek or even presume to demand a sign.' It is easy when things are difficult, or when we are perplexed and do not know which way to go, to seek a sign from God, and, in effect, to put him to the test in a way which is inconsistent with a firm trust in him and the sure promises of his Word.

AN IMPORTANT INSIGHT

We must begin by affirming that God himself does not put evil in our way. God has no hand in actually tempting us. We have cause to be grateful for the clear statement of the Letter of James: 'When tempted, no-one should say, "God is tempting me." For God cannot be tempted by evil, nor does he tempt anyone' (James 1:13). We are forbidden to call God in any sense, therefore, the author of our temptations. We may not place the blame for them upon him. He can never be tempted by evil, and he never tempts us to do evil. Rather an important source of temptation - and therefore, of sin - is our own evil desires (James 1:14).

God is sovereign, however, in what he permits to come into our lives. This request in the Lord's Prayer has in view his sanction which allows things to happen. No book in the Bible is more helpful here than Job. Many trials came to Job, and they were manipulated by Satan to become temptations to doubt God and to do evil. God permitted these things to happen, setting limits to how far Satan could go, having determined that Satan would overstretch himself, to Job's ultimate benefit and God's praise (Job 1:6-12; 2:1-10; 42:12). Job, however, could not see at the time what God was doing. It was only at the end that he could understand and witness what God finally brought about, and recognise God's compassion and mercy which had always been there (James 5:11).

Job's experience was not dissimilar from Abraham's. God tested Abraham's faith by delaying Isaac's coming into his and Sarah's life. Satan predictably caused that testing to become a temptation to doubt God, and to prompt Abraham to take things into his own hands. God's promise of a son and heir to Abraham by Sarah his wife had not materialised, and Sarah knew herself to be well past the normal age of child-bearing.

Abraham - using fallible human reason - recognised that God's promise of a multiplying family hinged upon his having an heir. Listening to Sarah rather than holding on to God's promise - and too no doubt not heeding his own conscience - Abraham fathered a son through Sarah's servant Hagar. Ishmael was the sad consequence of Abraham's yielding to that temptation, and the consequences were both sad and disastrous. But Abraham learnt his lesson. When later Isaac was born, and grew to manhood, God tested Abraham's faith by calling upon him to sacrifice Isaac (Genesis 22:1). God's careful testing of Abraham did not break him, but rather brought him to a spiritual summit, and to God's timely provision at just the right moment (Genesis 22:9-19). God did not test Abraham in order to find out about his faith, but in order to reward it.

Testing puts muscles on our soul; so God's people have found it throughout the centuries, sometimes to their surprise. John Newton expressed it well in a hymn:

I asked the Lord that I might grow
    In faith and love, and every grace,
Might more of his salvation know,
    And seek more earnestly his face.

'Twas he who taught me thus to pray.
    And he, I trust, has answered prayer:
But it has been in such a way
    As almost drove me to despair.

I hoped that in some favoured hour
    At once he'd answer my request;
And, by his love's constraining power,
    Subdue my sins, and give me rest.

Instead of this, he made me feel
    The hidden evils of my heart,
And let the angry powers of hell
    Assault my soul in every part.

Yea, more, with his own hand he seemed
    Intent to aggravate my woe,
Crossed all the fair designs I schemed,
    Blasted my gourds, and laid me low.

'Lord, why is this?' I trembling cried,
    'Wilt thou pursue thy worm to death?'
'Tis in this way' the Lord replied,
    'I answer prayer for grace and faith.

'These inward trials I employ,
    From self and pride to set thee free,
And break thy schemes of earthly joy,
    That thou may'st seek thy all in me.'

Testings are different from temptations in that Satan tempts to bring out the evil, but God tests to bring out the good. Satan tempts in order to destroy; God tests to prove our sincerity and increase our strength. Satan attacks when we are unsuspecting and unprepared; God never tests without providing a way of escape so that we may be able to bear all he permits (1 Corinthians 10:13; 2 Peter 2:9).

TEMPTATION ITSELF IS NOT NECESSARILY SIN

When we are tempted it is a considerable encouragement to recognise that temptation in itself is not sin, no matter how severely we are tempted: it is succumbing to the temptation that is sin. That statement needs one important qualification: it is sin to place ourselves deliberately in the place of temptation, perhaps because we enjoy its titillation as we play with it or because we are not determined enough in our desire to overcome it.

A group of travellers, including F. W. Boreham, a Baptist preacher, travelled through the Australian bush. They met a man who told them that he had just passed a python asleep in the undergrowth. Aflame with curiosity, they set out in search of it. 'It was not hard to find. Its fifteen feet of reptilian ugliness glistened in the sparkling sunshine. It was lost in the profoundest slumber - the long sleep that should have ended only with the spring. An exhibit in a museum could not have seemed more remote from life.' In hope of seeing some faint squirm or twitch, they tickled it and prodded it; they tried to lever up its head to get a better look at it. 'But,' to quote Boreham's description, 'we had carried our senseless liberties too far. The horrid creature woke up, not gradually, but suddenly, and turned savagely upon us. We scurried to the car as quickly as our legs would carry us, and when, on gaining that welcome retreat, we slammed the door behind us, the reptile already had his head upon the running board. For many nights after this adventure, we awoke in a cold perspiration, living once more through those tense and terrifying seconds and steadfastly resolving, in future, to let sleeping dogs - and other things - lie!' There is something of a parable there: we cannot help coming across temptations, but if we play around with them, they may prove to be our downfall.

If, for instance, one of our pre-conversion temptations, to which we regularly succumbed, was alcohol leading to drunkenness, we do not help ourselves by going to places or keeping company with those who put pressure on us to drink. Christians of all generations have recognised this. I enjoyed reading the somewhat unusual autobiography of Robert Flockhart, a Scot and British soldier, converted while in India, who became a gifted street preacher in the last century. While in India, he was invited after church to go for dinner to the home of one of the church office-bearers, the governor of the jail in Calcutta. 'On consideration, however,' Flockhart writes, 'I decided to refuse his friendly offer. I was but a young convert - my conscience was tender - I was afraid he would ask me to drink; that was my reason, and I was afraid of falling into sin. I was a "brand plucked out of the fire," and a brand, unlike a green stick, is easily rekindled. So I determined to decline the invitation, and went home to my own house rejoicing. The path of duty is the path of safety.' We cannot stop a bird choosing to land upon our head, but we can stop it making its nest there!

KEPT BY THE POWER OF GOD

In this prayer we recognise, first, that God is sovereign in what he allows to come into our lives, and that we need his help so that we do not let the testing become a temptation from Satan to do evil. This petition then is not a prayer to be kept **from** temptation but to be kept **in** temptation. We are asking, 'Do not allow us to be led into the power of temptation, where we may be caused to do evil and fall.' Or, put another way, 'Do not lead us into trials, even when necessary for our discipline, without your presence going with us, and your power keeping us.' An ancient Jewish evening prayer expresses the same thought: 'Lead my foot not into the power of sin, And bring me not into the power of iniquity, And not into the power of temptation, And not into the power of anything shameful.' The Syriac Liturgy of St. James also expands the petition helpfully to make its meaning clear: 'Lead us not into temptation which we, being without strength, are not able to bear, but also with the temptation make a way to bear it, and deliver us from evil through Jesus Christ.' We are not praying that we should not be tempted, but that we should not give in to sin's seductive allurements.

God never causes us to enter into temptation, but he does deliver us from it - as the second part of this petition teaches. We are encouraged to pray here for God's keeping power in times of testing and temptation. 'Watch and pray so that you will not fall into temptation,' the Lord Jesus urged his disciples in the Garden of Gethsemane (Matthew 26:41; Mark 14:38; Luke 22:40). If they had only kept awake and prayed this prayer that their Lord had already taught them, they would have alerted themselves to temptation's danger, and their need of God's help.

A purpose of our praying this petition is that we should constantly warn ourselves of temptation's reality and proximity, and our dependence upon our Heavenly Father's support to overcome it. To be forewarned is to be forearmed. Neglecting to pray this petition we are likely to forget the daily spiritual battle in which we are engaged.

Our conduct - here as elsewhere - is to correspond with our prayers. When we pray, 'Lead us not into temptation' we are not to put ourselves needlessly in its way. Offering this prayer sincerely, we will not readily fall into sexual immorality. To pray this prayer is to raise our spiritual and moral antenna or radar, and the Holy Spirit will see to it that we are then sensitive to the early approaches of impure and adulterous thoughts. Rather than playing with temptation we will run away from it as Joseph did. Going about his work conscientiously, he suddenly found himself alone with his employer's wife who urged him, 'Come to bed with me.' Although he refused, day after day she persisted. One day she caught him by his tunic and said, 'Come to bed with me!' Rather than argue, when no doubt passions were aroused, Joseph wisely ran out of the house leaving his tunic in her hand (Genesis 39:12). That action brought him into a lot of trouble as his master's wife falsely accused him of attempted rape. Although Joseph lost his job, he kept both his integrity and God's presence with him.

If we pray this prayer sincerely we will be watchful against sin's first approaches, whether through temptations to cut corners in business, compromise standards or keep quiet about our faith in our Saviour. I find that when I have sadly succumbed to a temptation, and confessed it, that it is helpful to ask God to make me super-sensitive the next time that same temptation makes its initial approach, so that I may nip it in the bud. Temptations are like weeds, they are so much easier to deal with in their beginnings than when given time to grow. God answers such prayer as his Spirit unfailingly reminds me of my request to God when temptation again raises its head.

If we pray this prayer sincerely we will be kept in the day of unusually fierce temptation. Sometimes temptation is not so consciously a problem, but there are other times when its force is almost unbelievable. Unexpectedly, it may be around the next corner, at whatever stage of life we are.

Temptations continue throughout life. Our fallen human nature, the wiles of the devil and the subtle - although sometimes blatant - attractions of the world see to that. Some temptations appear more potent at different stages of life, but every phase of life presents its unique temptations.

THE BEST OF EXAMPLES

Here as elsewhere our Lord Jesus is our best example. He knew the most severe temptations, and was the devil's number one target. The gospels record three specific temptations during his time in the wilderness. The first was that Jesus should demonstrate his Messiahship by meeting people's economic needs (Matthew 4:3), as the feeding of the five thousand, for example, showed he could have done if he had chosen (John 6:1-15). The second was that he should use startling and spectacular ways to win people's allegiance (Matthew 4:6). The third was that he should by-pass the Cross altogether and instead obtain authority and glory from the devil (Matthew 4:8,9).

Jesus assessed and answered the devil's tempting suggestions by the Scriptures - the Spirit's sword (Ephesians 6:17). The timely encouragement of the angels at the end of his period of temptation (Matthew

4:11) gives a clue to the intensity of the testing through which he passed.

That was not the end of the conflict, for it continued throughout the next three years. Jesus was frequently tempted to shrink from full obedience to his Father's will. The people regularly asked him for a spectacular sign as a ground for believing in his identity as the Messiah (Mark 8:11; John 2:18; 6:30). As the Cross drew nearer, the devil made temptation all the greater. But at the beginning Jesus showed the way he was determined to go. Together with recourse to the Scriptures, his first resort on every occasion was to seek his Father's face in prayer. When Satan placed temptation in his way at the feeding of the five thousand through the people wanting to make him king by force, he sent the disciples away, and withdrew to be alone with his Father (John 6:15), soon to re-emerge stronger than ever in his commitment to his sacrificial death (John 6:25-71).

In the Garden of Gethsemane Satan again exerted the full force of his evil powers against the Saviour, knowing that it was here that the battle was to be won or lost. Our Lord's answer was to pray. While he might have found physical relief through sleep - as the disciples did - the strength he needed was spiritual, not physical, and he found that as he prayed.

When we pray that we may not succumb to temptation, we are following our Lord's example in seeking our Father's assistance. If our Saviour needed to ask for help, how much more do we! As we ask our Father for strength, it is an unfailing encouragement to know we have at our Father's right hand our great High Priest who is able to sympathise with our weaknesses for he was 'tempted in every way, just as we are - yet was without sin.' (Hebrews 4:15).

Living in Scotland I have come to appreciate the Scottish Psalter and Paraphrases, and I particularly love the paraphrase of Hebrews 4:14ff:

> *Where high the heavenly temple stands,*
> *The house of God not made with hands,*
> *A great High Priest our nature wears,*
> *The Saviour of mankind appears.*

He who for men their surety stood,
And poured on earth his precious blood,
Pursues in heaven his mighty plan,
The Saviour and the Friend of man.

Though now ascended up on high,
He bends on earth a brother's eye;
Partaker of the human name,
He knows the frailty of our frame.

Our fellow-sufferer yet retains
A fellow-feeling of our pains,
And still remembers in the skies
His tears, his agonies, and cries.

In every pang that rends the heart,
The Man of Sorrows had a part;
He sympathizes with our grief,
And to the sufferer sends relief.

With boldness, therefore, at the throne
Let us make all our sorrows known;
And ask the aid of heavenly power
To help us in the evil hour.

Are we tempted to deny God? So was our Saviour. Are we tempted by the attractions of this world? So was he. Are we tempted to idolatry? So was he, for the devil tempted our Lord to worship him. Are we even tempted to kill ourselves? That was another temptation the devil threw at our Lord. As one eighteenth century preacher, Daniel Rowlands, quaintly but tellingly put it, 'The Head in heaven is sympathizing with the feet that are pinched and pressed on earth.' He is aware of our temptations as if he himself were in our position. The fellow-feeling he had with those in need while here upon earth, he has now in heaven (this is part of the significance of Hebrews 13:8). The prayer he put up for Peter is the prayer he prays for us: 'I have prayed for you, Simon, that your faith may not fail. And when you have turned back, strengthen your brothers' (Luke 22:32).

THE EVIL ONE

Up to this point we have indicated that temptations to evil originate particularly with Satan who finds an all too ready response from our fallen nature. This is confirmed by the second part of this petition, 'But deliver us from evil', which can be properly translated: 'But deliver us from the evil one.' (This petition is omitted by Luke.) The Bible makes no bones about the reality of evil in the world, and the personality of the one behind it. Satan, the evil one, is the god of this world, and the whole world is under his control (1 John 5:19). The evil one is twice called 'the tempter' in the New Testament (Matthew 4:3; 1 Thessalonians 3:5) or 'the tempting one'. But he appears often in that capacity without his title being mentioned.

He is like a lion always on the prowl (1 Peter 5:8), ferocious and totally indifferent to the well-being of his victims. He is said to roar because he is always on the warpath. He delights to catch us napping or off our guard. He has long experience as the tempter, and we are to take him seriously. Although defeated at the Cross, the devil is still active in the time left to him before the final judgment. Before new birth we belonged to him, and our evil actions gave proof of his ownership (1 John 3:12). But delivered from Satan's power by our Lord Jesus Christ, we are made strong to overcome him (1 John 2:13,14).

There are two extremes to avoid with regard to the evil one. The first is to neglect him, and the other is to be preoccupied with him. He delights in our going to either extreme, and we must avoid both.

To neglect him, and not to take him seriously, is one of the great mistakes of the Church. As Dr. Martyn Lloyd-Jones put it, 'There is nothing which is quite so disastrous as not to accept in its fulness the biblical teaching concerning the devil. I am certain that one of the main causes of the ill state of the Church today is the fact that the devil is being forgotten. All is attributed to us; we have all become so psychological in our attitude and thinking. We are ignorant of this great objective fact, the being, the existence of the devil, the adversary, the accuser, and his "fiery darts".'

After reading John Bunyan's *Grace Abounding,* Kenneth Macrae, a minister in the Free Church of Scotland, wrote in his diary, 'My perusal of this book has made me realise in some measure the deadness of that state into which I have come. I live as though Satan were a myth. Is it not high time to bestir myself out of this spiritual sloth lest I become a castaway? May the Lord have mercy upon me!' Later he wrote, 'I believe that I am too often taking to myself the responsibility for what is really the work of the Enemy and thus I am bringing myself into bondage because my conscience comes to be burdened with the guilt of such. We are not half aware of the reality of the work of Satan and of his extraordinary subtlety - I am not at any rate!'

The evil one knows the moments when we are most vulnerable. When he tempted Eve he came when Adam was absent and she was all alone. He chooses what is for him the best time to tempt us: when, for example, we are just converted; or when we are at a loose end; or when we are physically low; and even after some heart-warming time with God when we sense ourselves to be especially close to him, and well fed spiritually. The latter possibility may take us by surprise, but it should not. Is it not after a good meal that we are most inclined to fall asleep? If his identity was not so clearly delineated in the Bible, we would have to invent him in that his powers are so obvious in the world and in the Church. He prompted Judas to betray his Master, Ananias and Sapphira to lie to God, and Peter to deny his Lord.

Our lives are under constant attack from him. John Bunyan captured the reality of this conflict in his perceptive description of Christian's encounter with Apollyon (i.e. the evil one - see Revelation 9:11). Apollyon asked Christian, 'Whence come you? and whither are you bound?' 'I am come from the City of Destruction,' Christian replied, 'which is the place of all evil, and am going to the City of Zion.' 'By this I perceive that you are one of my subjects,' Apollyon responded. 'For all that country is mine, and I am the prince and god of it. How is it, then, that you have run away from your king? Were it not that I hope you may do me more service, I would strike you now, at one blow, to the ground.' Bunyan's narrative pinpoints the evil one's desire to have us back.

Satan's temptations and attacks come in a thousand and one ways. He gives us every encouragement to have double standards and to be hypocritical (1 Corinthians 5:8). He tempts us into error and extremes. He feeds any jealousy we have of one another, as he did in the case of Cain's envy of Abel (1 John 3:12). He loves us to be suspicious of each other, and to accuse one another (Revelation 12:10). We are not to be unaware of his schemes (2 Corinthians 2:11), therefore, and not least, so that we may be watchful and pray against them.

To go to the opposite extreme, on the other hand, and to become preoccupied with the evil one is one of the great follies of the Church. Some see devils, demons and evil spirits everywhere, in a way unsubstantiated by the Bible. Then God's people end up taking their eyes off our Lord Jesus, and, instead of rejoicing in his power and victory, they become preoccupied with Satan's power, and their own - often imagined - powers over him.

GUARDING THE GATES

The world, the flesh and the devil is the traditional summary of the sources of temptation, and it takes a lot of beating. Satan comes at us particularly through our senses. No one set this out more simply and effectively than John Bunyan in his book *The Holy War* in which the town of Mansoul has five gates: Ear-gate, Eye-gate, Mouth-gate, Nose-gate, and Feel-gate.

Our purpose must be to outwit Satan in the temptations he throws at us or into which he tries to entice us. We do this, first, by praying against him, as in this petition of the Lord's Prayer; and, secondly, by alerting ourselves to the ways in which temptations come, in order to be on our guard against him. This is the significance of the word 'watch' when our Lord Jesus urged his disciples, 'Watch and pray so that you will not fall into temptation. The spirit is willing, but the body is weak' (Matthew 26:41).

Watchfulness means identifying honestly the ways in which Satan most commonly comes at us so that we take preventative action where it is within our power to do so. The only danger in spelling out his most common schemes is that we must not imagine we know all his tactics. A benefit of the spiritual biographies the Bible provides - of people like Abraham, Sarah, Joseph, Moses, Samson, Saul, David, Solomon, Elijah, Elisha and the like - is that their lives reflect experiences of temptation common to all, for they were made of the same stuff as ourselves.

Abraham and Sarah were tempted to doubt God's promises - the promise of a son - and, as a result to take things into their own hands - hence Ishmael's birth. Joseph as a young man seems to have fallen into the snare of pride, as his father lavished unwise demonstrations of affection on him. Moses succumbed to the temptation to react angrily to the Israelites' stubbornness, and to go beyond what God commanded (Numbers 20:1-13) Samson was susceptible to the charms and attractions of the opposite sex. Saul gave in to the temptation to compromise his obedience to God. Job was tempted to curse God. David gave in to the temptation of pride as he numbered his forces to declare how vast they were, and he was tempted too by the physical attraction of someone of the opposite sex, a temptation compounded since she was already another man's wife. Significantly the temptation came in a moment of leisure when he was not occupied with his royal duties. Solomon, in spite of all his wisdom, succumbed to polygamy. Elijah was tempted to want to die (1 Kings 19:4); and so we could go on.

PINPOINTING THE MOST OBVIOUS TEMPTATIONS

Temptation number one - a temptation which lurks behind most others - is pride. Its potential danger is greater today because it may not even be regarded as a sin. We live in a culture where we are encouraged to feed our self-image and self-esteem by thinking always well of ourselves. By positive mental attitudes we are stimulated to be achievers. As with most errors there is a measure of truth behind this concept. We are to think well of ourselves in the sense that we were made in God's image and we are the objects of his love and grace. But we are not to think so well of ourselves that we do not face up to hard and sad truths about our fallen human nature, and our sinful inclination to think of ourselves more highly than we ought.

Satan works hard to encourage our sinful pride since pride was his own sin that brought his downfall. Pride is insidious. It leads us to think well of ourselves, and badly of others. It causes us to boast and to be arrogant, if not outwardly, inwardly. Unchecked, it creeps into everything we do, even corrupting what may seem to be the highest spiritual duties. John Berridge, a vicar of Everton in the eighteenth century, in a letter to John Newton described pride as the 'highest absurdity in our nature' and likened it to a hedgehog in that it rolls itself up as soon as we tackle it. All believers fight a battle against pride to the end of their lives. Writing to a friend, C. H. Spurgeon, the nineteenth century preacher, said, 'My Master is the only One who can humble me. My pride is so infernal that there is not a man on earth who can hold it in, and all their silly attempts are futile; but then my Master can do it, and he will. Sometimes, I get such a view of my own insignificance that I call myself all the fools in the world for even letting pride pass my door without frowning at him.' A hundred years later, Dr. Martyn Lloyd-Jones, acknowledged that the particular attack the devil made upon him was an appeal to his pride: 'Not my pride in the ministry but my carnal pride.' 'It was a terrible thing, it was the thing that revealed to me ultimately the pride of the human heart. I knew I was a sinner without any hope at all, but I never realised the depth of the pride of the human heart. Eventually I saw it was nothing but pride. Carnal, devilish pride. And I was humbled to the ground.'

Temptation number two is our sexual appetites. The standards of society inevitably place pressures upon us. Morality polls reveal statistics of people's new thinking on casual sex, affairs and pornography. A minority disapprove of immorality, and only a small fraction of men disapprove of calendars of naked women. The published opinion of some who hold high office is that drugs, pornographic magazines and casual sexual relationships are a matter of indifference, subject only to a person's choice and pleasure. Our sexual appetites may be easily stirred and quickly inflamed by the media and modern literature, obsessed as they are with sex. A literary critic recently confessed to not feeling good at having to review books which appeal to all our baser instincts. The media do not enhance our lives.

We probably need to be much more honest than we are about the way in which friendship between two people of the opposite sex can so quickly turn into sexual attraction and erotic love, not least when they share the same spiritual interest. C. S. Lewis was frank and forthright: 'When the two people who thus discover that they are on the same secret road are of different sexes, the friendship which arises between them will very easily pass - may indeed pass in the first half-hour - into erotic love. Indeed, unless they are physically repulsive to each other or unless one or both have already loves elsewhere, it is most certain to do so sooner or later.'

Although those of earlier generations may have been thought narrow, there was wisdom in avoiding too speedy a use of first names between the sexes, and putting a man or woman too close together in daily work.

Temptation number three is the imagination, one of the devil's favourite wrestling places. He knows how to tempt us deep within our being in ways none would guess, and without any other human being knowing. He is skilful in stirring up troublesome memories, thoughts and fantasies. Unhelpful things we may foolishly have watched, or even unintentionally seen in the past, he may present afresh to our minds.

Job was well aware of the snares that the use of his eyes presented. He was practical in dealing with his thoughts and imagination: 'I made a covenant with my eyes not to look lustfully at a girl' (31:1). Henry Martyn, one of the early British missionaries to India, put this into practice, when shortly before he sailed for India, he wrote in his journal: 'May 30. Went to India House. Kept the covenant with my eyes pretty well. Oh, what bitter experience have I had to teach me carefulness against temptation. I have found this method, which I have sometimes had recourse to, useful today, namely - that of praying in ejaculations for any particular person whose appearance might prove an occasion of sinful thoughts. After asking of God that she might be as pure and beautiful in her mind and heart as in body, and be a temple of the Holy

Ghost, consecrated to the service of God, for whose glory she was made, I dare not harbour a thought of the opposite tendency.' Imagination can be controlled, much as our sinful nature may suggest otherwise. Even as creatures of the dark in a cellar flee from the light as it is introduced, so as we allow the light of the Lord Jesus by his Spirit to flood our hearts and imaginations, evil things must flee.

Temptations may come at most surprising times and in seemingly unlikely circumstances. Satan has no respect for the spiritual or holy nature of our activities. He will attack us when we are worshipping God, praying, reading and meditating upon God's Word. He entered the Garden of Eden itself to attack Eve and then Adam. He took our Lord Jesus to the pinnacle of the Temple to tempt him.

AREAS OF ATTACK

Each petition in the Lord's Prayer represents an area in which the devil will aim to tempt us. He will try to sow doubts through questions. **Is God a loving Father?** No doubt Job found himself troubled by this typical assault of Satan when war and natural disaster took from him in one foul swoop both his children and his material assets (Job 1). Satan knows precisely how to aim his fiery darts when tragedy occurs or bereavement hits us.

Is holiness such a pressing priority? When we are in the company of other Christians or we are listening to the Bible being taught and preached, holiness is a glad, happy and privileged priority. But when we are perhaps strongly attracted to someone of the opposite sex, the devil's insinuations are subtle and insistent. 'Your standards are too high. You are being too hard on yourself. Let yourself go for a change!'

Is there really an everlasting kingdom to look forward to, and for which it is worthwhile renouncing the world's offer of the fleeting pleasures of sin? Suppose you are making a big mistake in putting so much confidence in the promise of the life to come? Think of what you are missing out on in the here and now when you decline to share in the activities your colleagues and neighbours consider so basic to happiness.

Is God's will good, and for our good? That kind of question is at its most subtle and powerful when perhaps an unmarried Christian is tempted to marry someone who is not yet a Christian. The heart's desires are often in danger of being more powerful than the head's reasoning. Satan sows the thought, 'You may be missing your last chance of marriage and of perfect happiness!'

Can we trust God to meet our daily material needs? The Lord Jesus teaches in the Sermon on the Mount and in this prayer - the Lord's Prayer - that we can, and we are instructed to pray for our daily bread. But Satan knows how to point us to the seeming security of material goals.

Is it really necessary to be sensitive to sin? The world at large is totally blasé about sin; so much so, that it scarcely uses the word. Satan knows how to make us feel old-fashioned and totally out of step with society whenever we use the word.

Do we literally have to forgive others if we are to be forgiven? Is that not taking things too far? Satan understands - better than we do - how damaging bitterness and an unforgiving spirit are in our relationship both with God and to others.

Many of these temptations - except that concerning forgiveness - were thrown at our Saviour by the devil.

We may see a relationship between this petition, 'Lead us not into temptation but deliver us from evil' and the petition, 'Forgive us our debts as we forgive our debtors.' A subtle temptation of Satan is to encourage us to think that God is not serious about linking our daily experience of his forgiveness with our forgiveness of others. Satan has been a liar from the beginning (John 8:44). The more forgiveness is deferred, the more difficult it becomes to implement. Furthermore, if we delay it, it becomes too easy to pretend that we have exaggerated the whole matter and that it is best forgotten. Not a few Christians fail to grow spiritually because of failure to admit to their need to forgive someone who has wronged them.

NO EXEMPTIONS OR RETIREMENT

There is no period in the Christian life when we are exempt from temptation. Those we experience early on in the Christian life may well be different from those we encounter later, but the spiritual battle continues to the end.

When I first became a Christian, I remember looking at the man who led me to faith in the Lord Jesus Christ - and he was twenty or so years older than I was - and thinking, 'When I get to his age, I won't have such a battle against temptation as I have now.' I was wrong! Old temptations remain as we get older, and each stage of life brings its own unique batch.

DELIVERANCE THE ORDER OF THE DAY

Our Father is sovereign over every attack of Satan, and deliverance is freely available through our Lord Jesus Christ. The Lord knows how to rescue godly men and women from trials and temptations (2 Peter 2:9). Satan would lead us into temptation; God would lead us out of it. He leads us out of it by a variety of means. First, he increasingly shows us the deceitfulness of our own hearts so that we admit that there are things that we need to run from, because we know that to play with them is as foolish as playing with matches and petrol. We are compelled to pray more - which can only be to our spiritual good - as we realise how vulnerable we are, and how dependent therefore upon our Saviour's delivering grace.

Second, he leads us out of temptation by incentives to holiness. We discover and prove that to resist temptation out of love for God brings us into deeper fellowship with him. The greater our fellowship with him, the more sensitive we become to the first approaches of temptation.

Third, he leads us out of temptation by providing ways of escape so that we may be able to bear and overcome it. The way of escape may be by his Spirit bringing to our minds a precept or promise of God, for such are effective weapons Satan cannot withstand. The way of escape may be a timely telephone call or letter from a Christian friend. The way of escape may be a reminder that our Saviour intercedes for us. The permutations of God-given ways of escape are beyond number; but they are always sufficient if we want him to lead and deliver us from temptation's power.

Fourth, he leads us out of temptation by calling off Satan. He can say to Satan, 'So far, but no further' even as was the case with Job (Job 1:12; 2:6). Satan's power is limited. God alone knows just how much we can take, and he will not allow us to be tempted beyond that limit (1 Corinthians 10:13).

Fifth, he leads us out of temptation by giving us strength to overcome, and to put Satan to flight. After our Lord Jesus was tempted, the angels came to minister to him (Matthew 4:11), and in the Garden of Gethsemane an angel came and strengthened him. When we resist Satan in the power God supplies, Satan flees from us (James 4:7).

God knows how to turn our temptations to our good. First, he uses them to keep before us our utter reliance upon the saving grace of our Lord Jesus. My temptations - their frequency and their surprising nature - humble me. How easily we become over-confident and presumptuous - and perilously vulnerable - if we forget the sinfulness of our heart. Secondly, he uses them to strengthen us spiritually. Temptations drive us to prayer, and to personal watchfulness. Thirdly, he causes us to appreciate our Lord Jesus more: how wonderful it is to know that at God's right hand we have One who was tempted in every way as we are, yet without sin. There is no one to whom I may run with such confidence, for both sympathy and help, than the Lord Jesus. Fourthly, by our experience of temptation, and God's gracious deliverance in them, we are better qualified to help others who are tempted.

We are further encouraged to pray this prayer because our Lord's special request to his Father, in what we sometimes call his High-Priestly prayer, was not that we should be taken out of the world, but that the Father would protect us from the evil one (John 17:15). In praying this prayer, 'Deliver us from the evil one,' we add our 'Amen' to our Saviour's request!

Praying this prayer, we raise the shield of faith with which we can extinguish all the evil one's fiery arrows (Ephesians 6:16). When Paul's messenger from Satan - his thorn in the flesh - entered his life, deliverance came as he prayed (2 Corinthians 12:7-10), and what Satan intended to be something to pull Paul down became a means of a unique discovery of Jesus' strength and power. It is by prayer that we put on our spiritual armour against temptation (Ephesians 6:10ff). As George Duffield's hymn puts it, 'Put on the gospel armour, Each piece put on with prayer.'

This prayer encourages us to be in no doubt of the identity of our enemy, and at the same time to know that he is to be overcome and that deliverance is always God's will for his children.

GUIDED TRAVELLERS AND GRATEFUL EX-PRISONERS

Guided travellers and grateful ex-prisoners are the seventh and eighth pictures that the Lord's Prayer provides of what it means to be a Christian: 'Lead us not into temptation but deliver us from the evil one.' Once we wanted to direct our own lives, but no longer. Once we were imprisoned by the evil one, but now we are free with the freedom with which God sets us at liberty in his Son. Given new life by his Spirit, we want to keep in step with the Spirit and walk in God's ways.

Chapter 8

A great treasure

'Yours is the kingdom and the power and the glory for ever. Amen'

I t is usual to conclude the Lord's Prayer with this ascription of praise to God. These words do not appear in the early Latin manuscripts, although they are found in the majority of Greek versions and are quoted by most of the Greek fathers, a group of early Christian writers, believed at one time to have had direct contact with some of the apostles. (They are sometimes called the 'Apostolic fathers' but it is a conventional title rather than an accurate one.) They frequently make reference in their writings to the books of the New Testament. In the Prayer Book of 1552 the Lord's Prayer is without the doxology, but it was included in 1662.

A SIGNIFICANT INCLUSION

The doxology's insertion is noteworthy in that it implies that from the early days of the Church Christians regularly added these words because they considered them an appropriate way to conclude the prayer. It fits in with other passages of Scripture, and is in total keeping with Paul's doxology, for example, in Romans 11:36: 'For from him and through him and to him are all things. To him be the glory for ever. Amen.'

THE UPWARD LOOK

Having begun the prayer with an upward look to our heavenly Father, we do well to conclude our prayers with our eyes upon him.

His is **the kingdom**. Rule and authority belong to him, so that we may be sure in all our prayers, that no matter how great the conflict with the evil one, our Father will have the last word.

His is **the power**. He 'is able to do immeasurably more than all we ask or imagine, according to his power that is at work within us' (Ephesians 3:20). Nothing short of his ability can grant the answers to the petitions we offer. He is able to do so much more than we can ever ask, or even think. He has done this in our salvation, a salvation that brings Jews and Gentiles together into one body and family. He has achieved glorious things for us personally and corporately. His power is beyond our asking: our petitions do not match it. His power is beyond our thinking: our thoughts do not tally with it. His power is already **within** us to do these things!

His is **the glory**. All credit, praise and honour belong to him 'in the church and in Christ Jesus throughout all generations for ever and ever!' (Ephesians 3:21).

If a chief benefit of salvation is adoption into God's family, our chief end is to glorify our Heavenly Father by lives that match the doxology of our lips.

AMEN

God's people are exhorted to express clearly and definitely their 'Amen' (Deuteronomy 27:15ff). The word itself has a long and honoured history both among Jewish people and in the Christian Church. When David first committed to Asaph and his associates what we know as Psalm 105 and they expressed its worship to God together, all said at the end 'Amen' (1 Chronicles 16:36). The last verse of Psalm 106 exhorts, 'Let all the people say, "Amen!"' (48). It was likewise the expected endorsement of the early Christians to public prayers (see, for example, 1 Corinthians 14:16).

Having listened to the chorus of blessing and honour ascribed to the Lamb who sits upon the throne for ever and ever, John in the Book of Revelation hears the elders say, 'Amen' (Revelation 5:14). If we are citizens of heaven, the strength of our 'Amens' ought to be a glad anticipation of the 'Amens' we will join in there. Jerome (340-420) says that in his day the congregation showed its approval of the sentiments and petitions expressed in prayer so enthusiastically that it sounded in the distance like a clap of thunder.

I was interested to read of an outsider's impression of an early Methodist meeting when the Wesleys organised believers together into small groups of men and women. 'Never,' he wrote, 'did I see or hear such evident marks of fervency in the service of God. At the close of every petition a serious **amen**, like a gentle, rushing sound of waters, ran thro' the whole audience, with such a solemn air as quite distinguished it from whatever of that nature I have heard attending the responses in the church service. If there be such a thing as heavenly music upon earth, I heard it there. If there be such enjoyment, such an attainment, as heaven upon earth, numbers in that society seemed to possess it.'

'Amen' is an expression of approval, by which we say, 'It ought to be so.' 'Amen' is also an indication of faith, for when we claim a promise of God, according to his will, we say, 'It shall be so.' 'Amen' is, furthermore, a declaration of desire, for often the prayer that is offered puts into words some deep longing after God himself, to which we say, 'Oh, that it may be so!' To say 'Amen' is a mark of agreement, and agreement is fundamental to effective corporate prayer. The Lord Jesus said that where two or three are agreed concerning anything which relates to his kingdom, they have their answer. Further, to say 'Amen' is a sign of earnestness, which is again an essential of true prayer (James 5:16-18). To say 'Amen' is also a indication of fellowship, an expression of our personal participation in the prayer that has been offered.

THE LORD JESUS IS THE AMEN

Some have not been drawn to the use of the Lord's Prayer because they have maintained that it is not a fully Christian prayer since it does not conclude with a reference to our Lord Jesus Christ. Such a conclusion is unjustified for three reasons. First, prayer in the name of the Lord Jesus was not to be a reality until after his atoning work. Secondly, the Lord Jesus would not have taught a prayer to his disciples that was to be renounced after Calvary. And, thirdly, Amen is his Name. God's promises in our Lord Jesus are 'Yes and Amen' (2 Corinthians 1:20). All that God encourages us to ask for - as in this prayer - comes to us solely through the redeeming work of his Son. We may say 'Amen' - 'So be it' - because everyone of God's purposes finds its fulfilment in our Lord Jesus Christ. Although at the time of the giving of the Lord's Prayer the disciples may not have grasped this glorious truth that the Lord Jesus is the Amen to our prayers, they certainly did after our Lord's death, resurrection and ascension! To say 'Amen' is to say 'For Christ's sake'.

A DELIGHTFUL COMPREHENSIVENESS

The Lord's Prayer gathers together all prayer's essential elements, with our major concerns being the honour of God's name, the coming of his kingdom and the doing of his will. These three preoccupations sum up our duty towards God.

The whole of our personal life is covered by its other requests: our past ('Forgive us our debts'), our present ('Give us our daily bread') and our future ('Lead us not into temptation').

The Lord's Prayer is like a ladder from earth to heaven. I find myself going through all kinds of moods, many of them quite inexplicable. Sometimes I feel elated as a child of God, other times I feel overwhelmed by my sin and the spiritual battle the Christian life involves. But the ladder never fails to help me, and once I place my feet on it, I begin to climb until I am rejoicing afresh in our heavenly Father's unfailing love and provision.

CHRISTIAN GROWTH

The Lord's Prayer provides a guide to healthy Christian growth. It is growth in our relationship to God our Father: we begin 'our Father'. We come to appreciate him more for all that he is in himself rather than for his gifts. Knowing his mind better, through growth in understanding of his Word, we become increasingly sensitive to both the things that please him and displease him; and we act accordingly.

Christian growth is progress in holiness: 'Hallowed be your Name'. Holiness is the unmistakeable goal God sets before us. Our sanctification will not be complete in this life, but will continue until the day we die or see the Lord Jesus Christ at his return - which ever takes place first. It is the particular task of the Holy Spirit, but a work in which he requires our co-operation as we are obedient to him. Many rough edges have to be smoothed, and attitudes changed. We are compelled to face up to uncomfortable truths about ourselves; but the acknowledgement of them, and the amendment that follows, bring progress in holiness.

Christian growth is enlargement in evangelistic and missionary concern: 'Your kingdom come'. This fits in so naturally with growth in our relationship with our Heavenly Father and with his Son, our Lord Jesus Christ. The closer we are to someone, the more we share that person's concerns and interests. The closer we are to God, the more we are aware of his concern for the world and of the compassion our Saviour feels for those who are as sheep without a shepherd.

Christian growth is increasing obedience: 'Your will be done.' As I grew up as a boy, I grew in my understanding of the kind of things that pleased my father. There came an indiscernible point where although I might not have talked with him about a subject, I could be certain what his reactions would be, because of my accumulated understanding of his viewpoint and preferences. As we know our Heavenly Father more, and especially through his Word, our greater knowledge brings a growing obedience.

Christian growth is the development of our dependence upon God: 'Give us today our daily bread.' Growing knowledge of God, and awareness of all that he is, increases our understanding of him as our Creator and Sustainer. As life unfolds, we discover how uncertain life itself is, and the daily perils that threaten us - dangers we little thought of when we were younger and perhaps starting out on our first job or career. Illness, accident and redundancy are daily happenings, and when they occur they sharpen our trust in God for our daily bread, and much else besides in ever-increasing areas of our life.

Christian growth is an increase in our sensitivity to sin and our desire to reflect God's likeness: 'Forgive us our debts, as we have forgiven our debtors.' A paradox of Christian growth is that the more we know God, and his Son Jesus Christ, the more conscious we become of our own sinfulness - and often in an overwhelming manner. We cry, with Paul, 'What a wretched man I am!' (Romans 7:24). The explanation is straightforward: the closer we are to a light the darker is our own shadow. We cannot get to know God better without his light showing up the dark areas of our life, and our realising how totally dependent we are upon his Son as our Mediator and Saviour.

Christian growth is progress in our desire for God's guidance, and deliverance from the evil one: 'Lead us not into temptation but deliver us from the evil one.' While once we might not have taken our vulnerability to temptation seriously, we do now - and increasingly so. Perhaps we once thought that temptation would decrease with age, but we have discovered otherwise. Whereas at one stage we might even have joked about Satan, we do not now for we know better. He is to be taken seriously, and so is our watchfulness against him.

A RECOVERY

The Lord's Prayer tends to be either neglected or ignored altogether in some parts of the Church, in great contrast to the practice of early centuries, where it was so highly valued that it was concealed from the outside world, and was reserved as 'the prayer of the faithful'.

Unhelpful repetitive use of the prayer, and a reluctance to use so called 'set prayers', may be part of the explanation. It has to be admitted that it may even sometimes have been used like a charm. But nothing should be allowed to rob us of its riches.

It is our Saviour's gift, and the distillation of his teaching on prayer. To offer its petitions is to pray in the will of God, and that is the heart of effective prayer. To be guided and influenced by its requests in our own petitions is essential if we are to pray in a way that pleases our Father. In a sermon on the phrase 'I called upon the Lord' (Psalm 118:5), Luther urged his congregation: "**Call** is what you have to learn. Don't just sit there by yourself or off to one side and hang your head, and shake it and gnaw your knuckles and worry and look for a way out, nothing on your mind except how bad **you** feel, how **you** hurt, what a poor guy you are. Get up, you lazy scamp! Down on your knees! Up with your hands and eyes toward heaven! Use a psalm or the Lord's prayer to cry out your distress to the Lord.'

PRACTICAL STEPS

How may we make better use of the Lord's Prayer in private and in public? Private daily use is helpful all the time we are able to pray its petitions meaningfully. If ever we feel that we are able to do so we should lay its use aside for a while.

I have sometimes found it helpful to stagger its petitions over the seven days of the week and to use each in turn as a stimulus to meditation and prayer. As a model for the proper priorities in our prayers it is always relevant:

Sunday
The honour of God's name in the world.
Monday
The extension of the Church through the preaching of the gospel, and the coming of God's kingdom.
Tuesday
The obedience of God's people to his will and his overruling control of all the events of the world.
Wednesday
Our daily practical needs and our work.
Thursday
Our relationships both with God and others, and their maintenance through the experience of forgiveness.
Friday
Our temptations and the spiritual battle in which all Christians are involved.
Saturday
Proper motivation - the honour and glory of God's name.

To pray the Lord's Prayer together in public is to remind ourselves that we are God's family, and that the prayer does not belong to us alone, but to all the members of the family. We need to be reminded of the family, and there can be little doubt that this was one of our Lord's reasons for providing it.

Traditionally, the Lord's Prayer has been prayed after another prayer or prayers, but there is no reason why we should not begin or end a service with it. From time to time it is beneficial to commence a service with the suggestion, 'Let's pray thoughtfully the words our Saviour taught us.' In early centuries of the Church it was sometimes used as an introduction to services of prayer.

The greater the variety of our pattern of use, the less inclined we will be to make its requests unthinkingly. If we use a modern translation of the Bible in church services, we will help the congregation if we pray in the words of that Bible version, perhaps pasting the words on the inside cover of our hymn or song books. This aids freshness, and a new generation will grow up knowing the contemporary version as well as many of us know its older forms.

A helpful variation is for the person leading in corporate prayer to use the Lord's Prayer sometimes as the framework for the prayers and intercessions of God's people, perhaps mentioning a petition at a time, pausing, and encouraging reflection on its relevance to contemporary situations, and then praying accordingly.

We will find it helpful to pray the Lord's Prayer in our homes when we are together as believers, and not least in some of the crises of life when we find ourselves lost for words.

A TALENT AND A JEWEL

Luke significantly follows the Lord's Prayer with our Lord's parable illustrating God's readiness to hear our prayers (Luke 11:5-8), with the assurance that he will respond more readily than any human father does to the requests of his children (Luke 11:11-13).

The Lord's Prayer is like a talent our Lord Jesus places into our hands to use well, not to be buried in oblivion, but constantly employed. Augustine (354-430) indicated that in his day new converts were taught this prayer at the time of their baptism, and were exhorted: 'Receive now this precious jewel and keep it; receive the prayer which God himself has taught us to bring to God.' That exhortation is relevant still. So let us pray this prayer, and value highly this precious and unique prayer model, the gift of our ascended Lord.